PHOTO COURTESY OF HAL BENDER, NBC

MISS AMERICA!

Delight thyself also in the Lord; and he shall give thee the desires of thine heart.

Psalm 37:4

A BRIGHT SHINING PLACE

THE STORY OF A MIRACLE

A BRIGHT SHINING PLACE

THE STORY OF A MIRACLE

by

CHERYL!

Miss America 1980

with

KATHRYN SLATTERY

Praise
BOOKS

A Division of Harrison House, Inc.
Tulsa, Oklahoma

Cover photo by Mario Casilli Photography, *courtesy of Archangel Motion Pictures and Television, Tulsa, Oklahoma.*

4th Printing

A Bright-Shining Place
ISBN 0-89274-460-X
(Formerly ISBN 0-385-17021-1)
Copyright © 1981 by Cheryl Prewitt-Salem
    and Kathryn Slattery
P. O. Box 701287
Tulsa, Oklahoma 74170

Published by Praise Books
A Division of Harrison House, Inc.
P. O. Box 35035
Tulsa, Oklahoma 74153

Permission to quote lyrics from the following songs is gratefully acknowledged:

From *Hand in Hand with Jesus*. Copyright 1940, © 1968 by Stamps-Baxter Music & Ptg. Co. All rights reserved. Used by permission.

From *It's Really Surprising (What the Lord Can Do)*. Copyright 1948, © 1976 by Albert E. Brumley & Sons. All rights reserved. Used by permission.

From *We Don't Cry Out Loud* a/k/a *Don't Cry Out Loud*. Lyrics and Music by Peter Allen and Carole Bayer Sager. © 1976 Irving Music, Inc., Woolnough Music, Inc., Begonia Melodies, Inc., & Unichappell Music, Inc. (BMI). All rights reserved. International Copyright secured.

A BRIGHT SHINING PLACE

THE STORY OF A MIRACLE

Contents

IT WAS SPRING, 1968, and already the air was warm and muggy. From the sound of the crickets, it looked to be a long summer. Locked in the heart of Mississippi, Choctaw County could get like a steam bath in the summertime; by the time coastal breezes from faraway places like Gulfport and Biloxi reached us, they were nothing more than worn-out sighs.

I was eleven years old, just finishing the fifth grade. Mother was in the kitchen fixing supper, while I was out front, sweeping the floor of our little country store.

The store took up the better part of the downstairs of our house, which used to be a Methodist church. Six years earlier, when a new church had been built, Daddy had bought the old white frame building, towed it a quarter mile down the road to its present site on State Highway 415, and renovated it for our family. Daddy was a contract carpenter, and he knew just what he wanted to do. Upstairs were the bedrooms and baths; downstairs were the kitchen, store, and music room. While Daddy worked during the day, Mother ran the store. My sixteen-year-old sister, Paulette, and I helped. Tim, our six-year-old brother, was too small to do much more than get in the way. Our other little brother, Heath, was just a baby.

Sweeping the floor may not have been one of my favorite chores, but it was part and parcel of being a Prewitt. Weekends and summertimes found me sweeping three and sometimes four times a day. That, plus keeping the tops of the canned goods dusted, the soda machine stocked, and the deep-freeze window clean so folks could get a clear view of our Fudgsicles and Eskimo Pies. Mother believed in keeping her store as clean as her house.

What I liked best were the times Daddy let me pump gas. Just beyond the screen door with the Dr. Pepper sign on it, we had two Gulf pumps out front. Motorists passing by on their way to and from nearby towns like Chester, Weir, and Ackerman often stopped at our place for groceries and a fill-up. Most of our customers were friends and kinfolk; lots of times I think they just liked to stop to visit.

"Hey, Cheryl!" was the way a typical customer might greet me, hopping out of his car and heading for the store. "Fill 'er up, and I'll meet you inside." Most of the roads around our parts weren't paved, and it took a lot of elbow grease to get the red clay dust off the windshield. That, plus checking the tires for air and the battery for water. I didn't mind, though. I liked to think how happy the customer would be when he saw the good job I'd done. Then, after filling his tank, I'd go inside the store to find him waiting for me, more than likely settled in one of our old wooden rockers—pack of Tom's Corn Cheez in one hand, can of Coke in the other—talking up a storm with Mother. Often, Mother looked relieved at my arrival; though she loved her customers dearly, she sometimes found them hindrances to keeping stock and bookkeeping. All I minded were the Corn Cheez crumbs left scattered all over the floor.

"Cheryl!" Mother called from the kitchen. "You finished sweeping?"

"Soon," I sniffed. The dust tickled my nose.

"When you're done," she said, "be sure to pick up your toys. Then come here and mind Heath for me. Daddy's coming home early tonight, and I've yet to make biscuits."

"Be right there."

I reached over and turned up the radio. The Blackwood Brothers were on the air, singing one of their gospel classics. Humming along, I joined in the chorus of "Hand in Hand with Jesus." I loved to sing. Loved to perform. Most of all, I loved to play the piano. I'd been playing since I was five, when—according to Mother and Daddy—I one day climbed up on the stool of our old upright and surprised everyone by playing by ear, with both hands, "When the Saints Go

Marching In." The only trouble was that I was a "lefty," playing melody with my left hand and accompaniment with my right. "Now see here, Carrie Lou," Grandma Prewitt had warned my mother, "don't let that girl grow up left-handed. What will happen when she starts to sewing? There are very few scissors for left-handed ladies." So while Mother worked to correct my left-handedness, I continued playing by ear. In third grade, I started lessons. Daddy said my talent was a special gift.

Now, listening to The Blackwood Brothers' soaring voices —their butter-smooth melody and razor-sharp harmony—a shiver of delight ran up my spine. I guess you might say The Blackwood Brothers were my musical idols. After all, this part of Mississippi was "Blackwood Country," home of the world's most famous gospel singing quartet. All the original brothers—Doyle, James, and Roy—had been born just a few miles down the road from us, east of the Natchez Trace Parkway. Though there were holes in the roof and the yard was a trangle of weeds and brambles, the old Blackwood homestead was still standing. We passed by it most every day. Daddy could remember before the Blackwoods were famous, back when they lived and worked as sons of a share-cropping farmer. Next time they had a concert nearby, he said that he'd take us to hear them sing.

This was especially exciting for Paulette, Tim, and me. For the past year, encouraged by Mother, the three of us had been singing together as a family gospel group at local churches, revivals, "singings," and singing schools. We called ourselves "The Prewitt Children," and some folks seemed to think we were pretty good. The original trio formed when I was five years old, and included me, Paulette, and our older cousin, Marsha. When we first started out, it was Marsha's parents, Uncle Lee and Aunt Evalee Prewitt, who carried us to all our singing engagements. Later on, Mother became more involved. Just last year, about the time Marsha became interested in boys and wanted to drop out of the group, Tim had been old enough to step in and take her place.

Singings and singing schools were old-time traditions in our part of the country. Singings were typically community events, taking place in local churches on Saturday and Sunday nights. Singing schools, however, operated on a larger scale, usually taking place in the summer and sometimes lasting as long as two weeks. During that time, whole families—grandparents and little kids alike—would convene daily for instruction in the rudiments of music and gospel singing. At the closing session, an all-day and evening affair, everyone attending had a chance to perform. Also, for anyone interested, there was the annual state singing convention—the grandaddy of Mississippi singings. Once, at a live broadcast from a state singing convention, we sang on the radio. *Truly*, I recall thinking on that day, *now we are stars*. The only trouble was that, though Mother supported our efforts, Daddy never wholeheartedly approved. He didn't mind us singing as a family in church, but he couldn't see the sense of us performing in public.

"Cheryl!"

Hastily, I turned off the radio and joined Mother in the kitchen.

"Here you go," she said, handing Heath over to me. "Poor little guy's been fussing all day." With the back of her hand, she wiped a stray wisp of hair from the side of her face. "Hot," she said. "Looks to be a long summer."

I nodded. Sitting cross-legged on the floor, I set Heath down to let him play. He was such a cute little baby—kind of fragile-looking, with wide brown eyes and big ears. I reached over to tickle him on the belly and he squealed with delight. The sound caused Mother to smile.

Even in a hot kitchen, hands and face dusty with flour, Mother was pretty. Even when she cried and especially when she laughed, her blue eyes sparkled in the nicest way. Of all of us, Mother, I think, was probably the most emotional.

Daddy, Hosea Amos Prewitt, was a big man—strong, authoritative, yet gentle. Folks around here called him Mr. Hosea. His broad, callused hands were equally at ease swinging a pickax or cradling a newborn baby. In fact, Daddy helped deliver all his children—including me! I once heard him say that the first time he laid eyes on me he did three things: prayed over me, committed me to the Lord, and dressed me in my first diaper. He said he did so well diapering that at one point the nurse got all confused. "What's wrong with this child that she never needs changing?" she asked. Daddy just laughed.

Both Mother and Daddy were born and raised in Choctaw County, children of Mississippi farmers. Both were from large families (four girls and three boys in each) and strongly Christian homes.

Mother's parents, John and Juanita Tennyson, still lived in the same house where Mother was born, seven miles away. Papa Tennyson often recalled the days when cotton was the area's big money crop, back before the boll weevil blight of 1912. "Shoot," he'd say, shaking his head, "I can remember when a good mule traded for forty acres, and thirty dollars kept a man's family fed for a year." In recent years, more and more families had left their farms for better-paying day jobs in the Delta. Folks owning wooded properties had sold out to the big paper companies. Still, Papa and Mama Tennyson had held on to their farm and land. Happily retired, with sixteen grandchildren and more on the way, they figured they'd done all right.

Daddy's folks, William and Viola Prewitt, also lived nearby. Every afternoon at four they could be counted on to stop by the store for a visit. Pa Prewitt was a man who, some might say, was set in his ways. With short skirts being the latest fashion, he sometimes gave Paulette a hard time. "But, Pa," she'd say, "times have changed." "Harrumph!" he'd exclaim, crossing his arms and frowning furiously at her hemline. "Not *that* much. Not *that many* inches!" Eventually, Paulette learned during Pa's visits to keep a low profile when wearing anything above the knee.

"Cheryl, honey," Mother spoke as she methodically cut biscuits from a half-inch-thick slab of dough. "Did you get your toys picked up? Mr. Horton makes a delivery tomorrow, and I wouldn't want him to trip over anything and get hurt."

"Yes," I answered. "Everything's put away."

Mr. Horton was our milkman. Short, cheerful, big around the middle—he reminded me a lot of Santa Claus. Back when I was six years old and we first opened the store, I used to love his visits. Twice a week he pulled up in his big shiny dairy truck, and without fail I was there to greet him. He never seemed to mind my nonstop chatter or the way I followed him around like a shadow. Together we loaded the store refrigerator with half-gallon plastic jugs of milk—whole, skim, 2 percent fat—and cartons of buttermilk, cream, and cheeses. All the while I asked him questions: "Why are there so many different kinds of milk? Are there different kinds of cows?" Or, "Why do they call it cottage cheese? Do they make it in little cottages?" Mr. Horton never lost his patience. He always did his best to answer. Then, before leaving, he'd often turn to me and say, "You know, little girl, some day you're going to be Miss America. You're my little miss today—but some day you're going to be the whole world's Miss America." "Really, Mr. Horton?" I'd ask. "Is that really true?" "Yep," he'd grin. "And don't you forget it." Then I'd reach up, hug his neck, and give him a great big kiss.

"Mother," I asked, "do you think it could ever come true—what Mr. Horton used to tell me?"

"What's that dear?"

"That I'd be Miss America some day."

"Goodness." Mother paused, wiping her hands on her apron. "He did say that, didn't he? Well—if *he* believes you can, I don't see why you can't. Believe hard enough, and a person can do most anything. That's what the Bible says." Holding the oven door open with one hand, she slid the sheet of biscuits in with the other. "There now," she said, shutting the door and reaching over to set the timer. "That's done. Why don't you set the table while I feed Heath? Daddy'll be home any minute. After supper, the Rays are coming over to sing."

"Oh, good!" I set Heath in his high chair.

Frank and Osie Mae Ray were neighbors, among our closest friends. They lived about a mile south of us, just across the holler, and once a week or so our families got together for an evening of singing and playing—mostly gospel music. Occasionally, Uncle Willie, Mr. Frank's brother, would join us, and then anything could happen. There was something about Uncle Willie's presence that caused all the men to slip away and sing the corniest old country songs, hillbilly-style. What a ruckus! Much as I loved Uncle Willie, I sure didn't favor that kind of music. Tonight, however, it would only be the Rays.

At the sound of car wheels on gravel, I was the first at the door to let them in.

"Hey there, sweet thing!" Mr. Frank picked me up off the floor and squeezed me tight. "Ready to sing?"

Not waiting for an answer, he put me down and extended a big hand to Daddy, who was standing beside me.

"Hosea," he said.

"Howdy, Frank."

Suddenly the house was filled with Rays and Prewitts of all ages, all hugging and kissing and laughing. "Kissin' kin," we called ourselves and, in fact, we were. Never could figure out exactly how; distant cousins most likely, somewhere back among Mother's and Mr. Frank's relations. One of these days we vowed to go down to the Choctaw County courthouse and poke around the archives to find out exactly how.

Daddy and Mr. Frank practically grew up together; they lived in houses a couple-hundred yards apart in the little town of Chester. They used to ride to school together in an old mule-drawn wagon. Now, Mr. Frank drove a gas truck for a living.

Mother and Miss Osie Mae were also well acquainted; for a while it seemed they were always having their babies near or at the same time. Cathy Ray was sixteen, the same age as Paulette. Though they were sophomores at different high schools (Cathy went to Ackerman, Paulette went to Weir), they were pretty good girl friends. Johnny Ray and I were also close in age, though he was a grade ahead of me. Both of us attended Weir School, but Johnny played mostly with the boys. Besides, Johnny was always talking about his big brother, Glendale. Recently wed, Glendale Ray and his new bride, Susan, were expected home for a visit the next weekend—a fact about which Johnny was very excited.

We walked through the store and back to the music room, where worn-out quilts hung on the walls for better sound. Some of the quilts had covered Mother's bed when she was a little girl.

We played and sang for maybe an hour or so—Daddy on guitar, Mr. Frank on fiddle, me on piano, and anyone who felt like it, singing. After trying some lively tunes, such as "I Saw the Light," and "O Happy Day," we rested in the peace of the more traditional hymns such as "Amazing Grace" and "How Great Thou Art."

But, as the evening wore on, it gradually became apparent that something wasn't quite right. For some unknown reason, our spirits seemed weary. From the start, Mother and Miss Osie Mae hadn't been singing; away in a corner, they were busy trying to comfort Heath, who had been crying off and on all night. And Paulette had claimed outright that she was tired; for the past week she hadn't been sleeping well, and the night before she had wakened, frightened by a bad dream. Something about a car wreck.

"Let's take a break," said Daddy, resting his guitar against the piano. "Better yet, let's call it a night."

No! I wanted to protest. But Daddy's set brow told me he'd made up his mind. There would be no more music tonight.

Frustrated, I left the piano and went over to the sofa where Paulette and Cathy were deep in conversation. One look told me I wasn't welcome. They must have been talking about boys.

Seated in the center of the big hooked rug that covered the floor, Tim and Johnny were arguing over a pair of toy trucks.

Mother and Miss Osie Mae had left the room, having gone upstairs to put Heath to bed.

Meanwhile, Daddy and Mr. Frank had pulled up chairs around the television and were watching the small screen intently. As black and white shadows flickered across their faces, they spoke in low tones. The program was a news special about Dr. Martin Luther King, Jr. A few weeks back he'd been killed on a hotel balcony in Memphis, and the whole country was still torn up about it.

"It's a terrible thing," I heard Daddy say. "A terrible thing."

Mr. Frank nodded.

"Hard to understand," said Daddy. "He was a God-fearing man."

Returning to the piano, I tried to amuse myself by picking out a few tunes. But I couldn't concentrate. *What was different about tonight?* I wondered. *What was wrong?* Closing the lid over the keyboard, I put away the songbooks. I couldn't tell if it was due to the program on television or just my mood, but for some strange reason I felt alone. Kind of help-less. As though something big was about to happen.

I shivered.

Something big was about to happen, and there was nothing I could do to stop it.

SATURDAY, MAY 4, had been hot and sunny. Now, in the early afternoon, great puffy clouds rolled across the sky and the sun played games of hide-and-seek. From the ravine that ran behind our house all the way out to the roadside in front, our yard was abloom with patches of red clover and blue and white wild flowers. Here and there, like buttons on a huge tufted quilt, big purple thistles nodded their heavy heads.

Out in the backyard I was busy stacking bricks to make the walls for a new doll's playhouse. Being a carpenter, Daddy always had lots of extra building supplies around— bricks, boards, cement blocks, and the like. *This*, I thought with satisfaction, *was destined to be one of my better creations*. Already there were three rooms, each with walls four bricks tall. Wearing my new plaid shorts and red shirt, I was doing my best not to get dirty.

Sitting on a blanket beside me was Heath. At thirteen months, Heath was at the age when everything—edible or not —appeared delicious. Now, to my dismay, he was happily sampling the shoulder of one of my favorite paper dolls.

"No!" I cried, rescuing the soggy figure and placing it behind me, out of Heath's sight. "Here, baby, take this." I placed on his lap a yellow cigar box that would later serve as a doll's bed. Next to playing the piano, playing with dolls was my most favorite thing.

Shading my eyes with my hand, I glanced up at the sky. Though clouds were building fast, their bases growing ominously dark, the sun had been shining brightly for the past few minutes. It felt good on my back. For a moment I felt like one of the turtles I'd so often watched, basking on logs along the banks of the creek that ran behind our house. *How fun to be a turtle*, I thought lazily—*to swim and sun and carry my house wherever I wanted* . . .

"Hey, Cheryl!"

I squinted up at Tim, breathless from running. My foot-high wall stood between us and, teasingly, he picked up one of the bricks as though to dismantle my work.

"Cut it out!" I yelled. "What do you want?"

"Paulette's going for a ride," he said, returning the brick to its proper place. "Going down to Chester to pick up some tomato plants. Mama said we could go."

For the past couple of weeks, Daddy, Mother, and Paulette had been planting our garden, a two-acre plot across the road. Planting was hard work, and Paulette had probably jumped at the chance to run an errand. Although she didn't have her license yet, she, like many of her friends, had been driving on our country roads for the past four years.

Sitting in the driver's seat, she honked the horn of our 1964 Chevrolet twice.

"Y'all coming or not?"

Picking up Heath and balancing him on my hip, I ran and joined Paulette in the front seat. Tim hopped in the back.

"Looks like one of Mother's friends has some good tomato plants for sale," said Paulette, as we pulled out of the driveway, made a sharp left, and headed down the hill that led to Chester. "Daddy wants to plant 'em late this afternoon. That way the sun won't scorch them before they have a chance to root."

"Oh," I said.

We'd driven about a mile when, up ahead, on our side of the two-lane dirt road, we noticed a car parked in front of Uncle Everett's house. Uncle Everett was one of Daddy's distant kin.

"Must be company," said Paulette. "I sure wish they wouldn't park in the road." Folks sitting in rockers on the front porch of the house were waving and smiling. I wondered at who.

"Guess I'll just have to go around," said Paulette. We were

traveling about thirty-five miles an hour when, in order to avoid the parked car, we crossed over to the left-hand side.

Suddenly, veering wildly, Paulette screamed. Coming toward us, full-speed, was another car. In one horrible moment of recognition we saw that it was the Rays—Mr. Frank and Osie Mae, Cathy and Johnny.

"*God, NO!*"

Cars were everywhere. There was no where for us to go. The last thing I remember was the expression of terror on Mr. Frank's face. That, and the sound of metal, glass, and my own scream.

"My God, my God. What have I done?"

Paulette was screaming. From the corner of my eye I watched as she struggled to pick up Heath, who was lying limp on the floorboard. Her face was covered with blood and her right arm hung at an odd angle. I tried to move, but I couldn't. My body was pinned between the crushed door and the fire wall which, with the engine, had been pushed onto my lap by the impact. I tried to move again and this time screamed with pain. I hurt everywhere—my back, chest, head, and—most of all—my leg. Something was terribly wrong with my left leg.

Glancing down, I felt sick at what I saw; from my knee to my hip, there appeared to be no bone. Slack, jellylike, the flesh surrounding my thigh had collapsed.

I screamed.

In the distance I heard echoes—the sounds of others in pain and agony. Worse were the cries of fear and despair.

"Where's Mama?" Cathy and Johnny were crying hysterically.

"My God," I heard Mr. Frank moan, "what's happened to Osie Mae?"

Wailing sirens announced the arrival of an ambulance, and

I watched as someone—I couldn't tell who—was placed on a stretcher and lifted into the back of the cab. Everyone, apparently, had been removed from the two cars but me.

The idea of being trapped in the car caused me to panic, but I was too weak to cry for help. Staring wildly up through the crazed glass of the shattered windshield, I noticed the sun had disappeared. A slight drizzle began to fall, and the rain felt cool as it mixed with the blood that was running down my face. I closed my eyes.

The next thing I saw was Daddy's stricken face as he kneeled on the driver's seat and gently touched my shoulder.

"Don't worry, honey," he said. "Everything's gonna be all right. Your door's stuck shut, so what I'm going to have to do is lift you over the back of the seat and take you out through the back door."

"Oh, Daddy," I cried. "Tell me I'm dreaming. Tell me this isn't happening."

Next thing I knew, he had me in his arms and was carrying me to a waiting car. The pain was unbearable. Again, I felt sick as I caught a glimpse of my left leg. Dangling limp over Daddy's strong forearm, it bent not at the knee, but at mid-thigh. It was horrible. Turning my head, I looked back at the two demolished cars. *How could anyone be alive?* I wondered. Staring down where tires had dug deep skid troughs in the dirt road, it occurred to me that red clay isn't red at all.

When we got to the car, Mother was sitting in the middle of the front seat, cradling Heath. Her face was ashen as she gently stroked his head, which had swollen to nearly half again its normal size. His little eyes had a funny glazed expression. Upon seeing me, Mother burst into tears.

"Carrie," said Daddy, "Carrie, it's gonna be all right."

Paulette was sitting next to Mother. The car door was still open and I noticed that one of her knees was bleeding badly. Looking again, I felt that now-familiar sick feeling as I saw that it had been nearly cut in half, with bone and tendons exposed.

Gently, Daddy lay me down in the back seat with Tim.

"Lost my front teeth!" he was wailing. "Lost both my teeth!"

Apart from that and a nasty bump on his forehead, he appeared to be all in one piece.

Our ride to the hospital in Eupora, a town nearly twenty miles away, was a nightmare. Daddy drove at breakneck speed, and every once in a while I could hear his voice above the engine as he spoke to Mother. The Rays, he explained, had gone to the hospital in Ackerman. That way, there would be enough doctors to take care of everyone. Osie Mae had gone in the ambulance.

After a while, everyone—even Heath—stopped screaming. A grim silence descended that was broken only by cries of pain caused by the motion of the car against broken and bleeding bodies. That, and Paulette's repeated and desperate plea:

"What have I done? Oh, God, what have I done?"

"Hush, child," said Mother softly. "You've done nothing wrong."

But there was no consoling her.

Once at Eupora's hospital, medics met us with stretchers and carried us to emergency and X-ray rooms. News of the wreck had traveled fast throughout the county, and it seemed that there were hundreds of people awaiting our arrival. Friends and relatives covered the grounds and lined the hallways. Because of our severe head injuries, none of us were allowed any pain-killers. Not even aspirin.

"I can't get all the glass out of this one," said one doctor as he worked on a three-and-a-half-inch gash above my right eye. "We'll have to sew it up the way it is."

"I can't say," I heard another doctor respond tersely to

Daddy, when asked about my leg. "It's a bad break, and I can't say if she'll ever walk again. I can't say much of anything. All we can do is try."

Paulette and I were assigned to the same room. After being X-rayed and stitched, I was put flat on my back in traction, unable to move any part of my body except my head. According to doctors, I had suffered a multiple fracture of my left thigh bone, four inches above the knee, lacerations of the head and face, and internal and back injuries.

Paulette had broken her right arm and had severed the main tendon on her left leg at the knee within an eighth of an inch. With all her walking around at the scene of the accident, doctors told her it was a miracle it hadn't snapped.

Tim had fared pretty well, having been initially knocked out and losing his two front teeth.

Heath, however, had suffered a much worse blow to his head, and doctors feared brain damage. In addition, at 11:00 P.M. the evening of the accident, it was discovered that he had broken his right leg.

Three days later, Mother was sitting between our two beds, quietly praying, when Heath's doctor came in. It was 10:00 P.M. In the semidarkness of the room, I listened to their conversation.

"Where's Hosea?" the doctor asked. His voice sounded concerned.

"Gone home for a little bit."

"When's he coming back?"

"Don't know for sure." Mother paused. "There's nothing wrong with Heath, is there?" she asked.

"Well, uh, yes," said the doctor haltingly. "We've got him in the X-ray room."

"What?" cried Mother. "Why? What's the matter with him?"

The doctor said nothing. Then, again, he asked, "When's Hosea coming back?"

"I *don't know*." Mother's voice choked with anxiety and exhaustion.

"Well then," said the doctor, "I guess then you'll have to be the one to help us."

"Help you?" asked Mother. "How? What is it you have to do?"

"It's too bad we didn't discover it earlier," explained the doctor, "but in the time that's passed since the accident, Heath's leg has started to mend crooked. In order to set it properly, we've got to pull it apart and break it again. We're shorthanded and need someone to hold the baby while we do it. I'm sorry, Carrie Lou."

Mother was crying as she left the room.

The next few days were a confusing blur of visitors, voices, and pain. Because of the extent of our injuries and the possibility of shock, doctors were afraid we might not live.

Sometimes, when we were alone, I turned my head and tried to catch Paulette's eye. But every time I made contact, she burst into tears. At some point it occurred to me that Paulette had taken blame for the accident upon herself; to look at me in my broken-up condition was more than she could bear.

The only person Paulette wanted to speak to was Daddy. Trouble was, every time she tried, she couldn't seem to get the words out.

"Daddy?" she'd begin.

"Yes, honey?" he'd respond.

Then she'd just look at him with the most tormented expression and start to cry.

It wasn't until we'd been in the hospital for a week that Paulette was finally able to ask the question that had been bottled up inside her since the day of the accident—a question whose answer she already knew, but refused to accept.

"Daddy," she said haltingly, "tell me about the Rays. What's happened? How are they? Tell me the truth."

"Well," said Daddy slowly, "as I think you know, Mr. Frank is doing fine. He lost his kneecap and had to have an operation, but doctors say he'll eventually be up and walking, good as new. Cathy's fine, too. She got cut up some and broke her leg, but doctors say it's nothing time won't heal. And Johnny—well, Johnny's fit as can be. Nothing wrong with Johnny. That little guy came through it all without a scratch."

Suddenly, Daddy was quiet.

Now, in the silence, Paulette—who had been hanging on to Daddy's every word—began to tremble. Her face paled. Her blue eyes clouded with fear.

"And Miss Osie Mae?" she whispered. "What about Miss Osie Mae?"

Pulling his chair closer to Paulette's bed, Daddy gently took hold of her hand.

"Honey," he said quietly, "I'm afraid what you've heard is true: Miss Osie Mae is dead."

"No!" cried Paulette, wrenching her hand away. "I won't believe it!"

"Now Paulette," said Daddy desperately, "I want you to listen to me, and I want you to listen good. First of all, you are not to blame; there's a rise in the road in front of Uncle Everett's place that no one ever noticed. There's no way possible that you—or anyone—could ever have seen that car coming. Secondly, the Lord was merciful in this; doctors say that Miss Osie Mae never knew what happened. They say she died before ever reaching the hospital."

But Paulette, her face contorted with unspeakable anguish, would not be comforted.

"Get out!" she screamed. "Get out and leave me alone!"

Daddy just stood there, his hands thrust deeply into the pockets of his overalls. Helpless, he watched as Paulette, her face turned toward the wall, refused to acknowledge his presence. Later, when he turned around to leave, I was amazed to see that his eyes were filled with tears. I'd never before seen Daddy cry.

Two weeks after the accident, everyone had gone home from the hospital but me. Dejectedly, I stared at the assorted cards and wilted flowers arranged on the shelf beside my bed. I was still in traction, my left leg elevated a good ten inches higher than the rest of me, and I was still unable to move any part of my body other than my head.

Between visits from friends and family, I spent a lot of time thinking about Miss Osie Mae. Sometimes I found it difficult to believe she had died. Other times, the reality of the wreck and of her death was so vivid that I wanted to both scream and cry at the same time. When that happened, I prayed; first for Miss Osie Mae, up in Heaven, and then for me—thanking God for letting me live through something so awful that it had taken the life of another. Sometimes I felt almost guilty for living. *Why*, I wondered, *should I have been spared?* But whenever I tried to figure it out, I couldn't get anywhere. It just didn't make sense.

I also spent a lot of time worrying about my leg. Something was wrong with it, but no one would talk to me about it. Whenever I asked Mother and Daddy, they just looked at each other and then back to me saying, "The doctors are doing the best they can, so don't you fret. It's just going to take some time." But from conversations among the nurses, I knew the traction wasn't working; the bone fragments weren't aligning properly and the swelling still hadn't gone down.

Once I heard Mother describing my X-rays to a visitor by saying, "It looks like someone took a hammer to her thigh-bone—like little bitty pieces of shattered glass." I also couldn't help but recall the comment made by one of the doctors to Daddy on the day of the accident implying that I might never walk again.

"Well, young lady, how're you doing today?"

Dr. Booth was standing at the foot of my bed. My elevated leg obscured my view of his body, and all I could see was his face. Dr. James Booth, Eupora's general surgeon, was an old family friend and had taken charge of my case. Tall and lanky, his bright, birdlike eyes twinkled behind his glasses. For some reason, he reminded me of the stork who's responsible for delivering babies.

"Well," I giggled. "I'm just fine. And you?"

"Great!" he responded. "And I've got some good news."

Then Dr. Booth informed me that I was going to be transferred to a hospital in Columbus, fifty miles away, where a special bone doctor was going to look at my leg and see what he could do. The doctor, an orthopedic surgeon named Dr. William Sanders was one of the best in all Mississippi. Dr. Booth said that he was very familiar with broken legs like mine, and an ambulance would be taking me to see him this afternoon.

The ride to Columbus was awful. My leg hurt so badly, it was all I could do to keep myself from screaming. Mother and Daddy came to see me later, and the three of us were together in my new hospital room when Dr. Sanders entered to explain what he planned to do.

First he explained how the femur (the bone I had broken) was the largest, strongest bone in the body, and one not easily broken. If the force that had shattered it had been received by any other part of my body, such as my head or chest, I would have been killed.

Then he explained how all the little pieces in the fracture spot had not, as Dr. Booth had hoped, aligned quite properly. What he planned to do in a three-hour operation was line the pieces up, insert a steel pin horizontally through my tibia (the larger of the two lower leg bones) below my knee, and surround it all with a plaster body cast. The pin would serve to hold all the surrounding muscles and bone in position and would be removed in approximately six weeks. The cast would remain for three or four months.

He went on to explain how the fractured area had already begun to fill in with clotted blood and new bone growth and how, after the cast had been set, a calcium "callus" (the Greek word for sleeve) would envelop the fractured area, cocoonlike, to form a new bone. Eventually, through a process known as Wolff's law, once I started walking again, the excess bone growth would wear away until what remained would be almost like the original bone. Dr. Sanders didn't think the break had affected the bone's growth line (in this case, the part of the bone near my knee where new growth originated). And I was past the age of overactive bone growth which sometimes causes in small children (whose legs haven't been set properly) the broken leg to be longer than the other. My full recovery was, however, admittedly at the mercy of innumerable complications that might or might not occur along the way—or later. Dr. Sanders hoped for the best.

The operation was scheduled for the next morning.

When I woke that afternoon, I was completely encased—from chest to toes on my left side and from chest to knee on my right—in an eighty-pound plaster-of-paris cast. A slim steel pin protruded on either side of my left knee. An eighteen-inch-long bar connected and separated my legs just above the knee; built into the cast, the bar would also be used by people who would be lifting me from place to place. A hole had been cut for elimination. There was really no need to wear any clothing. I was helpless—entirely dependent upon others for feeding, grooming, transportation. Still, it felt good to know that something had been done—that a decisive move had been made toward my recovery. I wiggled the toes on my right foot.

I couldn't wait to go home.

SITTING in the "up" position of my rented hospital bed, I'd been working for the past hour on a paint-by-number barnyard scene. It was mid-July. I was staying in my parents' downstairs bedroom, and the air was stifling hot. Doubting if a hurricane could penetrate the thickness of my body cast, I felt like a person trapped in a steam box. Only my toes appreciated the breeze being stirred by the small electric fan droning away on the windowsill.

Raising my hand to wipe my brow, my elbow glanced across my just completed No. 6 Red barn. To my dismay, the resulting smear traveled all the way across the barn's roof, through the No. 3 Green trees, and on up into the No. 2 Blue sky.

"Darn!"

Frustrated, I took the cardboard "canvas" and placed it, along with my brush and neatly numbered canisters of paint, on the seat of the wheelchair parked next to my bed.

I didn't like doing paint-by-number paintings, anyway. I thought they were tedious and unimaginative. But then, there was a lot about my life during the past seven weeks I didn't like. Bored, lonely, hot, helpless . . . I was unable to do anything—reach for a book, turn on the television, go to the bathroom—without calling for assistance. Most of all, I missed my music—especially playing the piano.

Not that I hadn't tried.

Over a month ago, with this in mind, I'd called for Arlene, our cousin who had agreed to stay with the family through the summer to help Mother while we recovered from our injuries. Obligingly she came, grabbed hold of the grip bar built into my cast, hauled me onto my wheelchair, and rolled me into the music room.

Due to the horizontal mold of my cast, I was unable to sit in the wheelchair like an ordinary person, but rested on the

seat at a rather precarious slant. Likewise, I discovered I was
unable to face the piano in ordinary playing position (both
my hands were too far away), so I asked Arlene to try
rolling me up alongside the instrument instead. This proved
even less satisfactory; while one of my hands was too close to
the keyboard, the other (flung across my chest) remained
too far. After trying a few more positions, it became clear
that the situation was hopeless. My piano playing days were
over—at least until I was released from my cast.

In addition, the cast was top-heavy and the slightest touch
—say, an affectionate pat on the knee—was enough to send me
flying. This made everyone extremely nervous; the last thing
we needed was another accident. For this reason all wheelchair expeditions had been limited to smooth terrain—inside
the house.

Looking out the window, I could see Tim playing among
the brick ruins of my doll's playhouse. I felt a pang of jealousy as I watched him, wearing nothing but shorts and
sneakers, running free in the sunshine.

Sighing, I picked at the lace ruffle bordering the pocket of
my specially made gown. The gown, a gift from Norma
Snead, was one of many reminders of how nice folks had
been to our family since the accident. Miss Norma, wife of
Dr. Sam Snead (Ackerman's chiropractor and a longtime
family friend), had gone to a lot of trouble to fashion for me
a complete body-cast wardrobe—a collection of dresses (most
of them get-well gifts from folks who didn't realize I
couldn't wear normal clothes) from which she had removed
the backs and attached strings so that they could fit around
my cast. And not only personal friends like Sam and Norma
Snead, but lots of folks—even strangers—had showed they
cared.

Cards and letters continued to come in from towns in
Choctaw County that I'd never heard of. "We are so sorry to
hear about the accident," they wrote. "Please know we are

praying for you." Some letters from churches were five pages long, carrying the signatures of entire congregations.

I'd always believed in the power of prayer, and for a long time after the wreck I joined with others in asking God for our healing. One day, however, I overheard a conversation between two men in the store that had since left me confused.

"There's no need for so many prayers," declared one man who was aware of the many letters we had received. "That's right," agreed the other. "Pray once, and that's all God needs. Pray more than once, and it's a sure sign you've got no faith."

I didn't want God to think I didn't have any faith, so lately, instead of praying for healing, I'd been thanking Him for my progress. Though there was something about this approach that bothered me, it was true that I did have a lot to be thankful for.

With each visit to the doctor's office, the outlook for my recovery seemed to grow more encouraging. Just as Dr. Sanders had hoped, we watched through X-rays as a cocoon of calcium began to form around my shattered bone. And just last week, I'd had my pin removed. Though it was a painful experience and I screamed and cried (using an ordinary pair of pliers and no anesthetic, Dr. Sanders had to turn the pin once or twice to loosen it before yanking it out), it was, in the end, another sign of progress.

Still, despite moments of optimism, my days were tinged with an ever-present restlessness and vague depression.

Paulette was a big worry. Cold, distant, untouchable—she had become a different person since the wreck. Seemingly emotionless, she rarely laughed or cried. With each passing day she retreated further into her own dark world of guilt and despair. Nothing any of us would do or say could shake her out of it. Even her injuries were slow to mend; her broken arm had had to be reset twice.

A few weeks earlier, the two of us had been passing time in the store, talking and listening to the radio, when a grizzly old man came in and asked where the vending machine was. I vaguely recognized him—an occasional customer whose perpetual expression was that of a person who'd just had a taste of sour milk. I hadn't seen him for a while, but on this particular day he looked as ornery as ever. Pointing to the machine, I resumed my conversation with Paulette and promptly forgot about him.

Suddenly, however, just as the man was about to leave, he surprised us both by spinning around, glaring at Paulette, and —clear out of the blue—spewing acidly, "Now why, girl, did you go kill Osie Mae? What's the matter with you anyway?"

Paulette, paralyzed by the man's words, stared at him in stunned disbelief. Then, fumbling for her crutches, she got up and hobbled to the kitchen.

With a triumphant snort, the old man left.

I didn't know what to do.

The next morning, while Arlene was getting me bathed and dressed, she asked me how I'd slept.

"Not well," I answered. "Folks were up and walking around all night long."

"I know," she said. "I'm sorry. It must have been midnight when I woke up and found Paulette was gone. I looked all over for her and finally discovered her down in the store, huddled in a corner, crying—real upset." Arlene paused. "Do you have any idea why?"

I told her about the episode with the man in the store.

"That explains a lot," said Arlene thoughtfully, "because Paulette was praying—"

"Well, that's good," I interrupted.

"No," said Arlene, shaking her head sadly. "It's not good. Not this time. Paulette was praying to die."

From that time on, not even assurances from the Rays themselves—who continued to be frequent visitors—could convince Paulette that she was not to feel guilty for what had happened. Most recently, Glendale Ray, the only member of the family who had not been involved in the wreck, had stopped by to visit.

A few days earlier, he said, the Rays had traveled to Philadelphia, Mississippi, to appear at the court hearing concerning the insurance settlement for the accident. To appear in court was mandatory; the hearing was part of the legal process necessary for settling the insurance claims.

"The lawyer called us into the judge's chambers," recalled Glendale. "Me, Johnny, Cathy, and Daddy. Daddy, of course, was still using his cane, and Cathy was on crutches. We all sat at a long table while the lawyer explained the accident in detail, from start to finish, for the judge. When it was all over, the judge—who had been listening very carefully—turned to Daddy and said, 'Well, Mr. Ray, I'd say you've got a pretty good case. If you'll find out how well Mr. Prewitt is fixed financially, we'll see what we can do.' Daddy, shocked at the judge's implications, just looked at him and said, 'No sir, you don't understand. Me and Hosea Prewitt are neighbors. Friends. We don't want anything from him but what the insurance pays.' "

Glendale grinned. "Can you imagine?" he asked. "I don't reckon that judge was used to dealing with families like ours."

But a hush had fallen over the room, and no one said a word. Mother was clearly misty-eyed, and Glendale looked embarrassed that his story had been cause for anyone to get emotional. Suddenly Daddy, with his customary wryness, spoke up.

"Well," he said dryly, "It's common knowledge you can't squeeze blood out of a turnip."

That broke the tension and everyone started chuckling and crying and hugging one another. Everyone, that is, but Paulette. She just couldn't see that between the Rays and the

Prewitts there was nothing to be forgiven; all that existed between the two families was the love that had been there from
the start.

Heath, too, remained cause for concern.

A few days after the accident he began to suffer intense
epileptic-like seizures, a result of the blow to his still-swollen
head. The spells seemed to follow a three-step pattern: first,
Heath would cry, which then caused him to not be able to
breathe, until finally, he passed out—at which point his invol-
untary nervous system took over, which once again allowed
him to breathe. Two and three times a day I could hear the
sound of his peculiar choked crying, which usually indicated
the onset of an attack. "Arlene!" Mother would call with
alarm, and a flurry of activity would follow as Arlene came
running to help Mother try to stop Heath from not breathing
to the point of passing out. In recent weeks they had tried
everything, from spanking him (which did absolutely no
good at all) to blowing on his face and splashing him with
water. Nothing seemed to help.

One afternoon I happened to be in the kitchen when one
of the seizures took place. It was horrible. Helpless, the three
of us watched as Heath's eyes rolled back and he began to
shudder and go rigid. Arlene did her best to make him comfortable, while Mother held his tongue so he wouldn't swal-
low it. We waited for what seemed like forever for him to go
limp, indicating he had passed out. On this day, however, it
didn't happen. Panicked, Mother and Arlene had to rush
Heath, stiff and blue, to the hospital. The doctor said they
made it just in time; minutes later, and Heath would have
died or suffered irreversible brain damage.

Since then, the doctor had put Heath on phenobarbital, a
depressant drug, to keep his brain waves slowed down, with
the hope of preventing further seizures. Trouble was, the
drug made Heath drowsy and sluggish and often caused him
—like a little drunk man—to stumble and fall, which made

him cry, which triggered another attack. Still, it was the best treatment the doctor could offer. He couldn't say how the drug would affect Heath's physical and mental development; he doubted, however, that he would ever be at the same level as other children his age.

Now, in the distance, I heard the slam of a car door and the slap of the screen door, as someone entered the store. From the delighted tone of Mother's voice, I could tell it was someone special.

Moments later, Arlene poked her curly head in the doorway.

"Hey, Cheryl," she said. "You got company."

"Who?" I asked, as she came over and began to clear my discarded paint-by-number supplies from the seat of my wheelchair.

"Aunt Dot," she replied.

"Aunt Dot!" I exclaimed. Aunt Dot was one of my favorite people.

"Yep," said Arlene, as she took hold of my grip bar and began to lift me onto the chair. "And she's brought you something."

"Brought me something?" I asked. "What?"

"Paint-by-number set," replied Arlene with a straight face.

"No!" I cried, and then, realizing she was joking, I began to laugh. Arlene started laughing too, and it was suddenly apparent to me that if we both didn't calm down, I was going to wind up on the floor.

"Arlene!" I squealed. "Be careful!"

But it was too late. In what seemed like a slow-motion movie, Arlene crumpled to the floor, taking me down with her. No one was hurt, and for a full minute the two of us just lay there, laughing too hard to move.

"*What* is going on?" Mother stood in the doorway. As she surmised our situation, I could hear her voice slide from alarm to relief. "Honestly," she sighed, lifting me enough to allow Arlene to slip out from beneath me, "I don't know what I'm going to do with you two. Now don't be much longer. Your Aunt Dot's in the store waiting to see you."

Aunt Dorothy Tennyson was my mother's brother James's wife. An administrator with the Mississippi school system, she and Uncle James lived in West Point, nearly fifty miles away. Sophisticated, articulate, fashionable—Aunt Dot had always been my idea of the ultimate cultured lady. Not that she was uppity; Aunt Dot had one of the most loving personalities of anyone I'd ever known. Ours was a special kind of relationship; perhaps it was because as yet she had no daughter of her own—I didn't know. But over the years, Aunt Dot and I had grown to be closer than sisters—more like best friends.

She was sitting quietly, talking with Mother, when Arlene rolled me into the music room. Upon seeing me, she jumped up, rushed to my side, and threw her arms around my cast. While happy to see her, I was also overcome by an unexpected sense of shame and sadness that she had to see me in such a pathetic state. For a moment I feared I might cry.

"Why Cheryl, honey," said Aunt Dot, standing back and taking me in from head to toe. "You're not looking half as badly as I expected. I am so happy to see you!"

"Me, too," I sniffed.

"Now, there," she said firmly, "this is too happy a time to spoil with tears. Your mother says you're doing great! She says the doctors are real pleased. And I can't believe you've had more than a hundred stitches. Where?" she asked. "Show me."

I pointed to the long, thin scar running down my forehead, and to the lesser lines on other parts of my face.

"Oh dear," said Aunt Dot. "So, I see. And this cast you're in—goodness, that seems to be a clumsy thing. It must be terribly hot." Her brow knit in concern. "What's it like?"

"Oh, it's not too bad," I began, with the intention of offering her my standard reply. But suddenly I stopped, realizing from her troubled expression that I wasn't fooling her. "Oh, Aunt Dot," I said, "it *is* terrible." And then, in a torrent of words, I told her about my boredom, loneliness, and discomfort. How I hated paint-by-number sets. How much I missed my music and playing the piano.

Finally, I told her how, though I tried to be optimistic, sometimes I was scared. Scared that God wasn't hearing my prayers. Scared that I was praying too much or too little. Scared that I might never walk again.

"Oh, honey," said Aunt Dot, "God hears your prayers. You can be sure about that. And the more you pray, the better!"

"Is that true?" I asked. I told her about the conversation I had overheard between the two men in the store.

"Yes," she replied emphatically, "it's true. Often times a single prayer is not enough. Remember the story Jesus tells us about the man who needed three loaves of bread in the middle of the night and pounded on his friend's door for help? 'Don't bother me!' his friend replied. 'I'm sleeping!' But the man's need was great and he wouldn't give up. He kept on pounding at his friend's door until finally he answered. Jesus explains that if friendship wasn't enough, the man's persistence would be enough to get his friend out of bed to give him all he needed [Luke 11: 5-10 paraphrased]."

"Well," I said doubtfully, "I don't know."

"Let me give you another example," said Aunt Dot, her brown eyes shining with enthusiasm. "When you were a little baby—oh, maybe six months old—I used to spend hours holding you on my lap, bouncing you up and down, and repeating my name. 'Dot, Dot, Dot,' I'd say. You hadn't started talking yet, and it was my hope that my name would be your first word. This went on for weeks—you were just a little bit of a thing, with peach-fuzz hair—but nothing happened. Finally, after playing with you in this manner for an entire afternoon, I had to go home. 'Bye-bye,' I said, as I handed you back to your mother. And you, with the most serious blue eyes I'd ever seen, looked back at me and said, 'Dot!' It was one of the biggest thrills of my life."

"Really?" I laughed.

"Really," said Aunt Dot. "Never give up—it's a lesson I never forgot." She smiled. "And *you're* the one who taught me.

"But enough of this." She beckoned to Arlene who was holding a big brown box, about the size of a toaster oven. "I came here today to bring you this gift. Uncle James and I thought it might be something you'd enjoy."

Arlene placed the box on my lap.

"I didn't bother to wrap it," said Aunt Dot. "I figured you'd want to get at it as quickly as possible." With the sharp end of a pair of scissors, she deftly slit the box down its taped middle and pulled back the flaps. "Here you go," she said. "It's all yours."

Peering into the box, I was surprised to see, surrounded by crumpled newspaper, what looked like a short piano keyboard, with an electric cord attached. It wasn't too heavy, and as I lifted it out from the packing, Aunt Dot pulled away the box.

"It's a little electric organ," she said excitedly. "Here—set it on your lap while I plug it in."

"Wow!" I exclaimed, as I touched with my index finger what appeared to be middle C on the keyboard. The clear, treble note seemed to fill the room. The tone lasted as long as I kept my finger on the key. I let my fingers run up and down the scale—slow and awkward at first; the organ had a different touch than our piano, and I was out of practice. Then, picking out a simple gospel melody with my right hand, I formed chords to go with it with my left.

"What's that?" Paulette had entered the room. Curious, she came over and examined the organ. I tried to hide my surprise when she pulled up a chair and joined Aunt Dot, Arlene, and me in an impromptu chorus of "Amazing Grace." Paulette loved to sing, and for a brief moment it was as though she forgot her unhappiness in the sheer pleasure of the experience.

From the corner of my eye, I noticed Mother and Daddy standing by the cash register watching us. Mother seemed very happy. Daddy looked unusually thoughtful. Later, after Aunt Dot had gone home, I observed the two of them sitting at the kitchen table, deep in conversation.

For the next week, not a day passed that I didn't spend hours playing my electric lap organ. Though the days were still hot, I was no longer bored or lonely. Music was something I was good at, and now—since it was the only thing I could do—I poured my heart into it. Though the organ was limited in that it didn't have a full-size keyboard, I was still able to use it to improve my finger dexterity, and to work out new and difficult passages of music. I especially enjoyed taking songs and transposing them into different and unusual keys. When engrossed in playing, it wasn't unusual for me to lose track of time, and Arlene often had to get my attention by resorting to unplugging me unawares.

"Hey!" I cried, one early evening as she did just that. "What's going on?"

"Supper's ready," she said. "And I think your Daddy's got an announcement to make."

Removing the organ from my lap and setting it on the floor, she rolled me into the kitchen. We arrived just as Tim had finished saying the blessing. The tabletop was a blur of hands and arms reaching for steaming portions of fried chicken, corn bread, fresh-picked field peas, okra, and sweet potatoes.

Once everyone's plates were filled, Daddy cleared his throat in a way that indicated he was about to say something very important.

"Your mother and I have been doing a lot of thinking and praying," he said, "about a subject we know is very important to all of you—and that's your singing. Now I know I've never been one to see much sense to your performing as a family group in public, but lately I've come to believe differently. It appears to me that that's God's music you're singing, with the talent He gave you. Gospel singing—if it's done in the right spirit, for the right reasons—can touch folks' hearts. It can lead them to the Lord. It can actually be a ministry. So, once your broken parts get mended, if you want to continue singing as The Prewitts, Mother and I will back you all the way."

Singing as The Prewitts had been about the farthest thing from my mind since the wreck. But now, at the thought of resuming our family group, I felt a flutter of excitement.

"I was talking to the preacher this afternoon," Daddy continued. "There's a revival this Thursday night, and he mentioned he could use a few good voices. I told him I'd ask you-all about it. What do you think?"

A chorus of approval went up from the table. Even Paulette looked up with a flicker of interest. I hadn't been outside the house all summer and the prospect of going to church—though the building was just across the street from us—seemed as big an adventure as a trip to Vicksburg.

The three of us spent the rest of the week rehearsing for our performance; we decided we would sing the old Stamps-Baxter songbook classic, "Hand in Hand with Jesus." Since I still was unable to play the piano, Daddy agreed to accompany us on guitar.

Thursday evening was hot and humid. As Arlene dressed me in one of my prettiest gowns and tied a ribbon in my hair to match, I felt giddy with anticipation. Too excited to join the rest of the family for supper, it was all I could do to drink my tea.

While Daddy set me gently in the back seat of our borrowed car, Mother rolled my wheelchair across the street to a waiting position at the top of the steps at the church. During the service, we sat in the back. When it came time for us to sing, Daddy rolled me up the aisle to the altar area in front.

Already, I was beginning to feel fatigued from the simple journey across the street. Still, as the preacher said a few introductory words, my heart was racing with excitement.

Then, he nodded his final go-ahead to Daddy.

"Well," said Daddy to the congregation, "I've not too much to say. Guess you-all know it's been a good while since we've all been able to be here together in church, and we're mighty grateful for this moment. Mighty grateful, too, for your prayers and concern these past few months. The young ones here have a song they'd like to sing that kind of says it all."

Stepping to the side, Daddy picked up his guitar and began to play our introduction. Looking out at the congregation—a sea of familiar and friendly faces—I felt my eyes well up with tears. Suddenly, it was all too much for me—the excitement, the physical exertion, the emotion of it all—and I began to cry.

All through our song I sobbed. I was unable to contain myself. And as we sang, the lyrics of the song broke through to me, their message of hope causing me to cry all the harder. Until now, I'd never before realized the personal nature of their promise:

> . . . In my night of dark despair,
> Jesus heard and answered pray'r,
> Now I'm *walking* free as air,
> Hand in hand with Jesus.
>
> Hand in hand we *walk* each day,
> Hand in hand along the way,
> *Walking* thus I cannot stray,
> Hand in hand with Jesus . . .

"I'm sorry," I said to Daddy, when it was all over and we were back home. "I'm sorry I cried, but I just couldn't help it."

"Oh, honey," he said. "You've nothing to be sorry for. You-all did a beautiful job, and I know it made God happy."

That night in bed, unable to sleep, I stayed awake for a long time. The moonlight through my window cast a tic-tac-toe-patterned shadow on the wall, and for a while I amused myself playing imaginary games with an invisible opponent. Finally I forfeited, never seeming able to remember where I'd placed my *x*'s and *o*'s.

Staring out the window, the trees were lit bright as day. I thought about my expedition to church. Though in one sense it had been a failure, it had been, overall, a glorious victory. Not only had I ventured outside the house, but I had done my favorite thing—perform, in my favorite place—church. The experience had made clear to me in a new way how much my music meant to me; to sing and play with the purpose of communicating the message of God's love was all I ever wanted to do.

At the same time, it occurred to me—with a startling sense of urgency—that if I was ever to attain this goal, I had to get well. I had no choice but to become strong and learn to walk again.

With this, I felt a twinge of fear. *What if I didn't get better? What if I never walked again?*

But then, I remembered what Aunt Dot had told me.

"Pray," she had said. "You can never pray too much."

I also remembered something else she had said . . .

"Never give up."

Another "school days" picture — not much improvement.

Now this is a pose! Body cast and all! Tim is here for moral support (and to make sure the wheelchair doesn't tip over!)

Now this look should give every girl in America hope for the future! Ha!

Oh! My best friend Doyle Blackwood.

What a clan! Mama's never in the picture because somebody has to be the photographer.

My senior picture!

Here I am with some of the kids I was teaching in singing school. (I was 15 years old at the time!)

Just me and my baby Heath!

College school picture. I must admit age agrees with me — there is some improvement.

First pageant, Miss Choctaw County. I was first runner-up!

This is the local Miss Starkville contest that took me all the way to Miss America!

Nice family picture! Ha! Mama, glad you could be in this one!

"UP YOU GO!"

Assisted by a strong-armed nurse, Dr. Booth hoisted me up onto the examining table in his Eupora clinic. It was a sweltering hot mid-August afternoon, and I was about to have my cast removed.

Two weeks earlier, during a visit to Dr. Sanders' office in Columbus, Mother and I had been told that recent X-rays indicated my leg had mended as much as we could hope for. Dr. Sanders had suggested that Dr. Booth be the one to remove my cast; that way, he explained, Mother and I would no longer have to travel all the way to Columbus. This had been fine with us, though we would miss Dr. Sanders, who, with his gentle manner and patient way of answering our many questions, had been a constant source of reassurance throughout the past three months.

Now, it was hard to believe that I'd soon be rid of my portable hotbox. The removal of my cast was an event I'd been looking forward to for what seemed like a lifetime. School would soon be starting, and I could hardly wait to begin the sixth grade like a normal person—free to see, touch, and move the lower half of my body, and free—hopefully—to eventually be able to walk and run like the other kids.

I glanced over at Mother, who was seated quietly by an open screened window. Restlessly, she clasped and unclasped the latch of her pocketbook. With anxious eyes, she watched as Dr. Booth traced on my cast with a black felt-tipped pen the line he would follow when cutting it open.

Turning my head toward the other side of the room, I noticed that the clock on the wall read 2:00 P.M. Watching as the red second hand swept silently around the clock's face, I listened to the squeak of Dr. Booth's pen and to the hum of katydids outside.

Suddenly, the sound of Dr. Booth's pen stopped. As I

looked up to see his smiling face, I also noticed the small electric buzz saw held in his upraised hand.

"Ready?" he asked.

"Now hold on just a minute," I grinned. "Let's not be hasty!"

"Now don't you worry about a thing," he said with a reassuring wink. "This won't hurt you a bit. What I plan to do is cut down the right side of your cast, and then down the left. After that, I'll do the same along the inside. Once that's done, we'll simply remove the top half of the cast—like the top of an old peanut shell—and then lift you out. Now, how's that sound?"

"Whatever you say," I replied. "But let's be careful— okay?"

But Dr. Booth, intent at the job at hand, said nothing. Instead, he nodded to the nurse, who came over and held my hand. It was her job to make sure I didn't move.

Suddenly, the lazy buzz of the katydids was drowned out by the shrill whine of the electric saw, and the acrid smell of burning plaster filled the room as Dr. Booth applied the spinning blade to the top edge of the cast, just below my right arm. I flinched, but the nurse held me still. Mother came over and took hold of my other hand.

In less than twenty minutes it was all over. With the help of the nurse, Dr. Booth tugged gently on the top half of the cast until, abruptly, it gave way. The cool rush of fresh air across the lower half of my body caused me to catch my breath.

"How's it look?" I asked.

No one seemed to hear me. Mother, I noticed, was biting her lip with concern, her eyes fixed fearfully on my legs. While Dr. Booth picked me up, the nurse removed the bottom half of the cast and propped it up in a corner. Free at last, I could hardly contain my excitement.

"Let me see!" I cried. "Let me see!"

Struggling to sit upright, I was surprised to find I barely had the strength.

"Here," said Dr. Booth, "let me help you. But Cheryl, honey, before I sit you up—before you look at your legs—I want to warn you that what you'll see won't be very pretty. But don't," he glanced at Mother, "let that worry you. It's perfectly natural for anything that's been concealed in a cast for three months to look downright nasty."

Then, being careful not to touch the ugly red bedsore that had formed on my right hip, he propped me up. For the first time in three months, I looked at my legs.

"Oh no," I murmured.

What I saw was shocking. Along with the cast, the top layer of skin had been stripped from both my legs. What was left was shriveled, dry, and mottled with patches of dried blood. Long, spidery stretchmarks traveled the length of my right thigh, where growth apparently had occurred—but my left leg remained weak, limp, and useless. For one horrible moment I wanted to crawl back into my cast forever, so hopeless seemed the prospect of ever walking again.

"Here," said Dr. Booth, offering me a pair of wooden crutches. "I want you to try these."

"Now?" I asked.

"Yes," he replied. "Carrie Lou here told me school's starting up in two weeks, and I imagine you'd like to be up and around by then, wouldn't you? Use these starting today, and in four or five months you'll be walking."

"Walking?" I asked, incredulously.

"That's right," smiled Dr. Booth.

With that, I reached for the crutches, which suddenly appeared to be two of the most beautiful objects I'd ever seen. Though at first they felt stiff and clumsy under my arms, after practicing with them for a few minutes, I was surprisingly mobile. A not so pleasant surprise, however, was the constant ache in my supposedly good right knee and spasmodic shooting pains that traveled from my lower back and hips to mid-spine.

When I asked Dr. Booth about my pains, he explained that my right knee had been badly twisted in the wreck and that the injury sustained by my back might be a problem for the rest of my life.

"Once you begin walking," he said, "you'll have to keep an eye on your knee. While the pain will eventually go away, the joint may have a tendency to go out on you. As far as your back is concerned, well, there's really not much we can do. Hopefully, in time, it will improve."

Still, my heart was singing as I hobbled out to the car with Mother who, with the nurse, carried the remains of my cast. I wanted to keep the thing—yellowed and useless as it was—as a reminder of how far I'd come.

The next two weeks were an exciting whirl of preparations for school; practicing the piano for my upcoming lessons, buying new shoes, selecting patterns and materials for clothes —and learning to balance on my crutches while Mother and Paulette took turns pinning my slacks, skirts, and dresses for hems.

The first time I stood for hems, the three of us made a rather startling discovery: my left leg, extended to its fullest, was a good two inches shorter than my right! While at first we found this alarming, after mentioning it to the doctors, we eventually adopted their hope that the problem was one that would remedy itself with exercise and time. Meanwhile, Mother would continue to hem my clothing to accommodate the difference.

On the night before the first day of school, before going to sleep, I thanked God for how far along He'd taken me in my healing; for the increased confidence and mobility He had provided through my crutches, and for all the hope and promise that the coming school year held.

Weir School (one of two schools in Choctaw County) included grades one through twelve, with an average of about thirty-five children in each grade. Teachers had been notified of my handicap, and arrangements had been made for me to be allowed extra time in getting from class to class and for front-of-the-room seating which would let me extend my left leg in the aisle. Friends had promised to help carry my books, and the gym teacher, Mr. DeWitt Cutts, had devised a special after-school weight training program that would help me regain my strength. More than anything else, however, I was excited about resuming my piano lessons with Mrs. Becky Curtis, the school's music teacher. Not only was Becky my favorite teacher, the lessons (two half-hour sessions a week) cost only $6.50 a month.

Gazing toward the far corner of my darkened bedroom, I could barely make out the ghostly form of my old body cast. I closed my eyes.

"Thank You, God," I prayed sleepily, "for everything. But please, God, don't let me fall down."

Falling down, as it turned out, was the least of my worries during the first few weeks of sixth grade. With my crutches and special privileges, I had become a sort of overnight celebrity—the center of attention; I loved every minute of it. Classmates vied to carry my books (which allowed them the fringe benefit of being late to class) and everyone, it seemed, wanted more than anything to either play with my crutches or hear, in gory detail, an in-depth telling of my accident (especially the part where Dr. Sanders had to pull the pin out of my leg).

Sixth-grade fame, however, I soon discovered was fleeting; it wasn't long before another student fell off a tractor and (with his ten stitches and Ace-bandaged ankle) into the limelight. With that, students no longer cared about hearing my story or playing with my crutches. Worse, friends no longer volunteered to carry my books. Often I had to ask for help in this area, and more than once—in the excitement of changing classes—the person forgot.

On one such October afternoon, as I was trying to get to my piano lesson, the tip of one of my crutches slipped on the edge of a step. Though I managed not to fall, my books went tumbling.

"Phooey!"

Now, I didn't know what to do.

If I set down my crutches to pick up my books, there would be no way for me to stand up again. Already, I was five minutes late for my lesson, my favorite part of the week. And I hated the thought of disappointing Becky, who meant everything in the world to me.

I first met Becky Curtis in the fifth grade, when she arrived at Weir School as one of the county's youngest teachers. Only nineteen years old and newly married, wearing a miniskirt and the latest bouffant hairdo, she was one of the prettiest ladies I'd ever seen—and so young! Not much older than Paulette. I don't know when I started calling her by her first name—it just sort of happened naturally.

Wanting very much to make a good impression at our first piano lesson, I had selected the most complicated gospel tune I knew and played it as hard and fancy as I could. When I had finished, Becky simply smiled and said, "That's very nice, Cheryl. Very nice. Now I'd like you to try and play this for me."

She placed on the piano the *John Thompson Songbook for Beginners* and opened it somewhere in the middle. The pages were black with notes, and my heart sank as I realized that Becky expected me to play the piece by reading the music. I didn't know how to read music. Even when playing in church or with the family, I had always played by ear. For a moment, I panicked, not knowing what to do. Then I hit upon an idea.

"Uh," I said, "you play it first, okay?"

"All right," agreed Becky. "Then you try it."

What Becky didn't know was that I had a very quick ear, and by hearing an arrangement just once, I was able to mimic it perfectly.

So Becky played, and I followed. She seemed very happy with my performance. This continued for about three or four lessons until one afternoon, upon opening the songbook, Becky refused to play.

"No," she said firmly, shaking her head, "not today. Today I want *you* to play first." She looked at me curiously.

Tears came to my eyes as I realized that my ruse had been revealed. "I can't," I said. "I don't know how. Oh, Becky, please don't be disappointed in me!"

"Now Cheryl, honey," said Becky, leaving her seat to sit next to me on the bench. "I'm not disappointed in you—why, I think it's wonderful the way you play by ear." She wrapped her arm around me. "But it's important that you learn to read music, too. Very important. You see, Cheryl, you are a very gifted little girl, and playing by ear can only take you so far. Why, there's a whole world of music out there just waiting for you to explore—but you must be able to read in order to find it."

Then she played me some samples of different kinds of music; classical, pop, country, jazz—rhythms and melodies I'd never heard. It was terribly exciting, and from that moment on, I vowed that I would learn to read music. Music was what I loved more than anything else in the world and I wanted to be able to do it all, and do it well. That hunger, plus my desire to please Becky, resulted in a year of musical training and growth more exciting than I'd ever known.

"Always have a goal," was Becky's motto, "and once you've reached it, set another. And remember, no matter how good you get, never be satisfied. Never! Because once you're satisfied, you have nowhere to go but down. If you're always striving to meet a new goal, you're certain to grow."

Encouraged by Becky, I was soon able to sight-read—that is, able to look at a page of notes and hear the melody and feel the beat in my head. Just as she had promised, a whole new world opened up for me; and the more I learned, the more I realized there was to discover.

Once, when I tried to explain my excitement about this to Daddy, he just shook his head and frowned. "Don't know or care much about those other kinds of music," he said. "But I do know gospel music belongs to the Lord."

While I wished that he understood, his sentiment was fine with me. With The Prewitts accepting more and more concert bookings, gospel music remained my personal favorite, too.

At present, however, none of this mattered very much. All I cared about was finding a way to pick up my scattered books and get to my lesson.

Suddenly I heard the clickety-click of heels on the corridor and Becky's voice, high and clear.

"Hey there, honey! What're you up to? I've been waiting for you!"

"I know," I said glumly.

"Here," she said, reaching down to pick up my books, "let me help. I've been looking all over for you, you know. I've got some big news!"

"News?" I asked. "What?"

"I'll tell you later," said Becky, "when we get to the music room."

Once there, Becky shut the door behind us. As I sat down at the piano, an old yellow-ivoried upright, she took my crutches and set them against the wall.

"Cheryl," she said, "you're familiar with our school's choral program, aren't you?"

"Yes," I answered. "Why?"

For many years, Weir School had had no formal choral program; occasionally preachers' wives might visit to teach group singing, but that's about all. With Becky's arrival, however, high-school-age students had been selected to form the Weir High Girls' Sextet, Boys' Quartet, Mixed Quartet, and (for anyone interested) the volunteer Mixed Ensemble. The selected groups competed in statewide festivals with other high schools and were fast gaining in reputation. Paulette sang in the Girls' Sextet and sometimes got to miss school when there were out-of-town competitions. I envied her on those days; it all seemed so glamorous and grown-up to me.

"Well," said Becky, her brown eyes twinkling mischievously, "the reason I ask, is because I've been thinking about starting you as piano accompanist for the Girls' Sextet. I know you're a lot younger than the other girls, but you've got a good ear and lots of experience. What do you think?"

"Oh, Becky," I cried, thrilled at the challenge, "I know I can! I just know I can! Just give me the music, and I'll practice real hard, and—"

"I know you can, too," said Becky, laughing. "And I think it'll be a lot of fun for you, also."

Our first competition was in Kosciusko, a town some thirty miles away. Becky, Paulette, and I selected the pattern and material for our and the group's ensemble outfits: brown double-breasted coat dresses, with white collars and cuffs. The three of us drove all the way to Columbus to find shoes at Butler's: brown patent pumps with white bows—and one-inch heels! It was the first time I'd ever worn something other than socks and saddle oxfords, and it took some talking before Mother was convinced that I should wear the heels. To be sure, it was unusual for a high school accompanist to be as young as I was; fortunately, I had the height, if not the figure, of a teenager. Still, in order to more fully look the part, it would be necessary for me to wear makeup—a little rouge, mascara, and lipstick. It took even more talking to convince Mother of this, and when she finally agreed, it was with the stipulation that we not let Daddy know. Thus, with our first festival in Kosciusko, Paulette and I began what soon became a ritual of arriving at Becky's house early to apply makeup and stopping there before returning home to wipe it off. From the start, I loved being with the older girls; it made me feel confident, capable, grown-up. Occasionally boys would be at the competitions, and I sometimes caught them looking at me out of the corner of their eyes. I liked that, too.

The school year passed quickly, and by late December, I was walking.

While this represented a tremendous milestone and was a miracle for which our family rejoiced, being able to walk did not mark quite the return to normalcy that I had hoped for. With or without crutches, I was still severely crippled. The difference in length between my two legs had not improved, and my limping steps were painful, slow, and awkward. The pain in my back also remained a stubborn problem, and I began to visit Dr. Snead for periodic chiropractic treatments.

At some point, it occurred to me that over the course of the school year I had, in a sense, come to be living in two very different worlds. Whenever I was home or in some way involved with music (either performing with the family or accompanying the Sextet with Becky), I felt wonderful—loved, accepted, relaxed, and happy. Thankfully, that was most of the time. School, however, was another story.

Though my grades were good and teachers friendly, I was sometimes overwhelmed with feelings of being left out by the other kids. Because of my handicap, it seemed that I was always late—and last—for everything: last to class, last to the lunchroom, and—worst of all—last to be selected for teams in gym. I never told anyone about my feelings—not even my best girl friend, Angela Kelley, the principal's daughter. Sometimes my feelings welled up inside me until I thought I'd burst. When this happened, I usually headed for the gymnasium, where I vent my frustration by working out extra hard on the special weight training program Mr. Cutts had developed for me.

But one spring day, while dressed in shorts and working out with two- and three-pound dumbbells, I glanced over at the gym door windows to see a gaggle of boys, their faces pressed flat against the glass, gaping and laughing at me. Though I knew the boys meant no harm (after all, I was a funny sight—not unlike the skinny fellow in the back pages of comics who's forever getting sand kicked in his face!) I was very embarrassed. From then on, I felt more comfortable at home, practicing the piano or playing with my dolls.

Toward the end of the school year, we spent our gym classes learning how to square dance. Though I wasn't very good at the dancing, I did enjoy the toe-tapping music and the confusion and fun that resulted when the beat really got to moving, and the step-caller began sounding like a tobacco auctioneer. More than once I fell down—but other kids did, too, so it wasn't so bad.

It was a Friday afternoon in late May, when Mr. Cutts announced that a school-wide square dance contest would be taking place in one week's time. Winners would be judged for originality and skill in two areas: dance and music. Rehearsals would start the following Monday, and everyone would participate.

Mr. Cutts had already divided the class into teams, and now, as he called out names and corresponding team numbers, I watched as kids scurried across the blacktop to join their waiting friends.

I was in Group Three. Though my last name began with the letter P and was called somewhere in middle, I was, as usual, the last to arrive. Trying to ignore the sidelong glances being cast between my team members as I made my awkward approach, I suddenly overheard someone whispering, "No fair! With Cheryl on our team, we'll never win!"

The words stung like fire, and I could feel hot tears filling my eyes. Then the bell rang and the groups dispersed, each falling into cliques of three and four and each, I was certain, talking about me.

"Hey, Cheryl!" It was my friend Angela, who was also on my team. "Isn't this neat?" she asked breathlessly. "I can't wait till Monday, when we start rehearsals. Aren't you excited?"

"Not really," I replied.

The truth was, I was dreading it. All I wanted to do was get home.

Once there, I didn't even stop in the store to say hello to Mother, but headed straight for the music room. Sitting down at the piano, I poured myself into the keyboard with a ferocity I'd never known. Letting out all my frustrations, all my hurts, I lapsed into what was most familiar to me and set about to playing every gospel tune I'd ever known.

I must have been playing for an hour or so, when Mother poked her head in the doorway and asked, "Cheryl, honey, is there anything wrong?"

"No," I replied, not bothering to look up.

For a moment, Mother was quiet. Then, before leaving, she said, "I finished sewing some new dresses for you today. Tonight, after supper, we can pin them for hems."

"Fine," I said curtly. I felt badly for the tone to my voice, but I didn't care about the dresses. I didn't care about pinning hems to accommodate my uneven legs. I didn't care about anything other than how miserable I was and how much I wanted to be like other kids, who never had to think about such things.

My thoughts turned to the afternoon's gym class, to Mr. Cutts's announcement about the square dance contest, and to Monday's upcoming rehearsal.

To me, the situation seemed impossible. How could I, with my crippled leg, be anything more than a burden to my team? Nothing anyone could do or say could help remedy this situation. Nothing.

My dark mood, I observed wryly, was in sharp contrast to the bright gospel melody I was pounding out on the piano. Curious, I glanced at the title: "It's Really Surprising What the Lord Can Do." And as I started to read the lyrics, I was surprised to find that I began to feel better—somehow more hopeful, more optimistic. This, I realized, was what Daddy loved so much about gospel music; sincerely believing the words, he took their message to heart. Suddenly, I stopped playing, and sang the words *a cappella:*

> If you are burdened down with care,
>   Take it to Jesus Christ in prayer . . .
> He can give gladness day and night,
>   He can change darkness into light . . .
> When you are lost and cannot see,
>   Jesus will hear your feeble plea . . .
> Blessings He gives to one and all,
>   Who on His precious name will call,
> It's really surprising—
> Really surprising—
> What the Lord can do—
> What the Lord can do . . .

Of course! I thought, when I had finished singing. *How could I have been so blind? God had helped me in the past; why, then, couldn't He help me now?* Closing the songbook, I shut my eyes and lowered my head.

"God," I prayed quietly, "You know better than I do about my problem in gym class, about my feelings of being left out. But according to this song and to what I know it says in the Bible, nothing is impossible for You. Nothing! So I'm praying now that You take hold of this impossible situation of mine and turn it around into something good—something surprising! Do that, and I promise to give You all the credit. Amen."

I didn't feel too much better after praying, but it was a relief to at least have gotten the problem off my shoulders.

Again, my thoughts returned to the dance contest. Reaching down to the floor where I had placed my notebook, I pulled out the mimeographed sheet that Mr. Cutts had passed out at the beginning of class. The white page, with its purple printed message, smelled faintly of ink. "Weir School Square Dance Contest," I read. "Winners to be judged for originality and skill in two categories: Dance and Music."

As I read the last line a second time, my heart gave a little jump.

Music! One of the major categories was music! Maybe here was a way I could help our team. While I wasn't much use as a dancer, when it came to music, I knew I had a lot to offer.

"Oh, thank You, God," I murmured, as I left the piano and ran over to the old wooden chest where stacks of music books were stored. In addition to gospel selections were a few classical, popular, and traditional pieces. Leafing through the songbooks, a tattered volume of *American Family Favorites* caught my eye. Listed in its contents was "Turkey in the Straw."

Perfect! I thought, as I set the open book on the piano and played a few bars. The familiarity and faintly comical nature to the tune made me smile. The more I played, the more clearly I saw in my mind's eye, a big old Tom turkey, scratching and strutting his way in time to the music. Letting my imagination go, I could almost see the barn, smell the musty sweetness of fresh-mowed hay. Almost before I knew it, my turkey had changed into a square dancer, surrounded by a circle of other dancers, all clapping, and stamping their feet and taking turns in center ring. . . . With a little work,

I was certain that "Turkey in the Straw" could be developed into a winning entry for the school competition.

For the remainder of the evening and on into the weekend, I continued practicing "Turkey in the Straw." By Sunday evening I had expanded it to accommodate an eight-minute dance that incorporated all the basic moves we had learned in class, plus some funny novelty steps that emulated turkey movements. Now, instead of dreading Monday's first rehearsal, I could hardly wait.

Early the next morning I caught up with Angela before school started and shared my idea with her.

"Wow, Cheryl," she responded enthusiastically, "that's great! We can tell the other kids about it this afternoon and see what they think." Then, her eyes clouded with concern. "But Cheryl," she said, "this is pretty fancy stuff, you know. It'll take a lot of practice, and—"

"I know what you're thinking," I interrupted. "I know I'm not very good at dancing. But why couldn't I play the piano? I could be the team's accompanist."

"Yeah," said Angela thoughtfully, "that's true. Let's ask Mr. Cutts and see what he says."

Not only did Mr. Cutts agree to the arrangement, but later that afternoon, when I presented my "Turkey in the Straw" dance idea to team members, it was met with whoops and hollers of approval. I could hardly believe my ears. With only four days remaining until the contest, we spent the rest of the afternoon practicing. From the start, it was clear that we were a real team, and for the first time in months I felt like my old self—accepted, useful, happy. Heady with the thrill of competing, I wanted more than anything else in the world for us to win.

On the day of the contest, after our group had performed, I really didn't know what to expect. Having had to concentrate on the music, I'd only been able to catch glimpses of the group in action. Mostly (as Becky had coached me to do so many times before for the Sextet competitions) I just smiled. I smiled so hard, I thought my jaw might drop off. Smiling was the one thing I could do to help us win.

Though we had been the second-to-last group to perform, my heart was still racing from the experience as Mr. Cutts cleared his throat in preparation for the announcement of winners.

"First place," he beamed, "for originality and skill in dance and, especially, music, is—Group Three!"

Us! We had won!

A cry went up from the team.

"Y'all did a bang-up job, kids," Mr. Cutts continued. "Congratulations."

Still reeling from the announcement, I wasn't prepared for what happened next. Suddenly I felt myself being surrounded by a throng of team members who, led by Angela, were shouting, "Three cheers for Cheryl—hip, hip, hooray! Hip, hip, hooray! Hip, hip, hooray!" Tears of joy streamed down my face and I heard myself cheering right along with the others. It was one of the happiest moments I'd ever known.

Later that afternoon, when I was home setting the table for supper, it occurred to me that I had experienced three things that day that I would not soon forget: first was the thrill of competing; second was the indescribable joy of winning; third, and most important, was the certain knowledge that with God's help even the most hopeless situation can be transformed into a victory! How many times in the past I had heard Daddy quote from the Bible, "All things are possible to him who believes" (Mark 9:23). At last, I understood.

As I folded a paper napkin and anchored it in place with a fork, I knew, in a new way, that if I was willing to try my hardest, whatever the task might be, God would always honor my efforts; that He was a loving God who wanted for me—as He wanted for all His children—nothing less than the best.

IT WAS a breezy March afternoon, and I was singing softly to myself as I walked along the red dirt road that led from the bus stop to home. Pausing to pry a large pebble from its clay bed, I gave it a good kick with the toe of my shoe. Running ahead some twenty feet to catch up with it, I kicked it again.

In the eighth grade now, my limp was barely noticeable. Though my left leg remained two inches shorter than my right, and Mother still hemmed all my clothes to accommodate the difference, I'd developed a cute little way of walking (a "priss," Daddy called it) that disguised my handicap so well that newcomers to Choctaw County never knew I had a problem. Besides, except when visiting Dr. Snead for back treatments, I rarely thought about my leg or the accident anymore. Mostly I spent my time thinking about music, school, and—most recently—boys.

Today I was feeling particularly cheerful. With summer just around the corner, it would soon be time to plant our garden and begin booking appearances as The Prewitts for upcoming church revivals, summer sings, and the like.

Upon arriving at our front door, however, my high spirits disintegrated like a wind-swept dandelion puff. Coming from within the house, I could hear the all-too-familiar sounds of Mother's and Paulette's dismayed voices and Heath's hysterical crying.

Heath was having another attack.

Though more than two years had passed since the accident, Heath's seizures remained severe and frequent. Still on daily doses of phenobarbital, his mental and physical growth had been markedly stunted; at over three years of age, he weighed only twenty pounds, and his poor coordination and dull expression betrayed his retardation. Doctors offered little hope that Heath would ever be normal, and handling his seizures—horrible as they were—had become a grim sort of routine procedure for all members of the family. For Paulette, they also served as an ongoing reminder of the wreck; a continual source of guilt.

"Can I help?" I asked, as I entered the kitchen.

"You're a little late," snapped Paulette. She was holding Heath, who, having already turned blue and collapsed, was now breathing again. "I'm sorry," she said, handing the baby over to me. "But sometimes this really gets me down."

"That's okay," I said, taking Heath in my arms. "I understand."

Though the afternoon was warm, Paulette was wearing—as she had for the past two years—long sleeves. Convinced that her broken right arm had mended crooked, she refused to wear anything else. (As far as everyone else could see, her arm had mended just fine.) But the issue was more than one of vanity for Paulette; she dreaded the possibility that the sight of her exposed arm might serve as a reminder to others of the wreck.

Paulette had had a difficult time of it, all right. Though her dark days of contemplating suicide had passed, she had continued to grow increasingly cold and withdrawn. Sometimes her deep unhappiness manifested itself in rebellion; by staying out late or flaring up for no apparent reason. When it came to dating, it seemed (to Mother and Daddy's dismay) that she was constantly involved in one tumultuous relationship after another. And though she had been graduated from high school for nearly a year and most of her friends had either married or gone on to college, she still had no clear plans for the future. What disturbed me most about Paulette was the fact that—though she smiled as broadly as any of us when performing—she seemed to have no emotions. She never laughed. She never cried. It was as though since the wreck, a large part of her had died, and nothing any of us would do or say could touch whatever small part of her remained warm and alive.

Suddenly feeling very tired, I sat Heath next to Mother at the kitchen table, surrounded him with his favorite toys, and headed upstairs. Intending to change out of my school clothes, I opened my closet door and reached to the top shelf where my T-shirts were stacked. There, to the left of the T-shirts, was my cardboard box of paper dolls.

Though I knew it was childish, I still played with my dolls; a vast collection of cut-out figures with outfits for every occasion, which Mother first began ordering for me from the Sears catalog when I was five years old. Next to playing the piano, playing with my dolls was my favorite pastime. Lately, however, my doll games had been changing —from "family," with mother, daddy and baby dolls, to "dates," with girl and boy dolls. If anyone ever found out I was doing such things, I think I would have died of embarrassment; for this reason I kept both my dolls and game-playing well-hidden.

Now, standing on tiptoes, I reached for the box and set it softly on the floor. I closed my bedroom door. I picked up the box and carried it to the far side of my room, on the far side of my bed—out of sight from any unexpected visitors. As I sat cross-legged on the floor and opened the box, I wondered what my friends would think if they could see me. The last time I'd played dolls with Angela had been in the sixth grade. "Aw, let's go do something else," she had suggested a short while later. "This is baby stuff." Angela was right. I was too old for dolls.

I was grown-up looking at fourteen, and more than once Mother had commented that I had sprouted fast. Though I wasn't allowed to date, I did have boyfriends. And even Daddy allowed me to wear a little lipstick now and then.

Still, there was something about my dolls that remained irresistible—especially on days like today that were trying and stressful. My last links to childhood, I couldn't let them go.

Reaching for my favorite boy and girl doll, I dressed them in their finest Sunday outfits. Just as I was about to have the girl doll refuse to kiss the boy doll (after all, it was their first date), Mother called to me from downstairs where she was minding the store.

"Cheryl?"

At the sound of her voice, I jumped.

"Can you come down here?" she called. "We need some help."

"Be right down!" I yelped. Guiltily, I swept the dolls back into their box and shoved them under the bed.

Running down the stairs, I was surprised to see that the store was fairly full of people. Business, since the building of Ackerman's new shopping center, hadn't been too brisk lately; Mother had taken to sewing for friends to bring in some extra money. But now there were six or seven customers, folks that had stopped on their way home from work to pick up last-minute items for supper. After tending to their needs, I noticed an old family friend sitting in one of the wooden rockers. A regular customer, he stopped by most every afternoon to relax with a Coke and pack of peanuts before heading home.

"Well, howdy!" I said, running over to the man and, as I had done so many times before, throwing my arms around his neck and planting a big kiss on his leathery cheek.

But this time, something was different. The expression on the man's face . . . the way his hand lingered on my hip. . . . Something was wrong. All wrong. Startled, I pulled myself away.

"I've, uh, gotta go," I stammered, hoping he wouldn't detect my mounting panic. "Gotta go get supper ready." I could feel the man's eyes watching me as I walked away. Once out of his sight, I fairly flew up the stairs.

Shutting my bedroom door, I sat down on the edge of my bed and tried to sort my rushing thoughts. *What had happened? Why had the man looked at me that way? What was wrong? I'd hugged and kissed him like that hundreds of times before. . . . Why did things have to change? Why couldn't everything stay the same?* I felt confused, frightened, angry.

Reaching under my bed, I pulled out my box of dolls. *My dolls were my friends,* I thought. *Reliable, unchanging, cooperative; they wouldn't cast me odd glances or cause me to be scared.*

But, as I spread the dolls out on the bed, it was as though for the first time, I saw them as they really were—flimsy, worn, and fake. Why had I never seen it before? Picking one up, it fell back, limp, in my hand. It was a doll; nothing more, nothing less. And suddenly it, and all its companions, had very little to do with me.

Anguished, I pushed the doll aside and began to cry. I was growing up, I realized, and there was nothing I could do to stop it. I didn't know exactly what growing up implied, but I did know that no longer could I sit on grown men's laps and win their affection with hugs and kisses. Moreover, no longer could I play with dolls.

"Please God," I cried quietly, as I stacked the dolls—figures in one pile, outfits in another—and put the lid on the box, "help me understand what's happening to me."

There was something about the moment that reminded me of the time Daddy and I had buried a baby robin that had fallen from its nest.

Still crying, I placed the box high, out of sight, in the farthest corner of my closet. I would never play with my dolls again.

That evening at supper I noticed that Daddy seemed unusually intense as he said the blessing. Glancing over at his bowed head, I was surprised to see how gray he had become over the past two years; his hair, once dark and close-cropped, now lay silver and smoothly parted. Mother, too, had aged; her thin hands, clasped in prayer, looked more like her mother's than her own.

Later that night, when we turned off the television and gathered in the music room to read scripture (a habit we had begun some time after the accident), Daddy fell strangely silent. As we took turns reading, he seemed to be lost in another world—and sometimes I saw him turning in his Bible to passages other than those that were being read. Just as Tim had closed us in prayer and we were all about to get up and leave, Daddy raised his hand.

"Hold it," he said. "There's something I've yet to say."

I glanced at Mother, who seemed as surprised at Daddy's words as the rest of us.

"I've been doing a lot of thinking and praying lately," said Daddy, "about a matter that touches all our hearts—and that's our baby boy, Heath. For two years, now, he's been suffering like no child should with those spells of his, and it's high time they stopped."

"But Daddy," I said, "you know what the doctors say. There's nothing we can do."

"Yes, I know what the doctors say," replied Daddy, "but the Lord's told me different."

"*What?*" Mother looked alarmed.

"The Lord told you?" asked Paulette. "What does that mean?"

We weren't used to hearing Daddy talk that way, and it made me feel very uncomfortable.

But Daddy, nonplussed by our less than supportive reaction, continued.

"The Lord told me to take that child off his medicine," he said. "And that's what we're going to do."

"No, Hosea!" cried Mother. "Are you out of your head?"

Paulette and I looked at each other. Never had we heard Mother speak to Daddy in that way.

"We're taking Heath off his medicine," repeated Daddy firmly. "And I don't want to hear any more about it."

Standing up, he closed his Bible and set it on the seat of his empty rocker.

"Time for bed," he said. "Good night."

Mother followed him out of the room, and as they walked away I listened to the sound of her questioning voice, high and excited, countered by Daddy's replies, low and deliberate. For nearly an hour their discussion continued; I was in bed when it finally stopped.

In the silence that followed, I tried to figure out what Daddy had meant by saying "the Lord told me." Whenever I said my prayers, I never received any personal replies. I also wondered what Heath's fate would be without his medicine. Before taking phenobarbital, his attacks had been so bad that three times he had almost died. Still, Daddy had seemed so certain of his decision . . .

The next morning was Saturday, and everyone was clearly edgy as we found our places around the breakfast table. Heath, propped up in his high chair, looked the same as usual, the only exception being his eyes; freed from the sedative effects of the drug, they appeared unusually bright. Hungry, he banged on the metal tray with his spoon. Then, to our alarm, he began to cry.

In a flash, Mother was by his side, stroking his head and murmuring soothing words. But this time his crying was different—not the peculiar choked sound that usually precipitated an attack, but the healthy wail of a hungry child. Still wanting more after finishing two steaming bowls of oatmeal, Heath went on to gobble up my unfinished biscuit and Mother's eggs. It was the most any of us could recall him eating at one meal. And when we tucked him into bed that evening the day had passed without him having an attack.

In like manner, three days passed, then a week, then three weeks. Still no one commented too much about Heath's apparent progress. Between all of us (with the exception of Daddy) there remained an uneasy silence about the subject; the prospect of his recovery seemed just too good to be true.

By summer's arrival, however, it was clear that Heath—like the plants in our garden—was flourishing. Having gained ten pounds, he was beginning to walk, and—as though wanting desperately to make up for lost time—chattering all the day long in an effort to talk. When Mother and I brought him to Dr. Booth for a checkup, the doctor was amazed.

"I can't figure it," he said, shaking his head. "If Heath continues improving at this rate, in a year or two he'll be back to normal. But I'll tell you one thing, Carrie Lou: if this here was my child, I'd never have had the nerve to do what you folks did. No way. Tell me, what put it in your head to take him off his medicine?"

"Oh," replied Mother, lamely, "you know Hosea. Once he makes up his mind on something, there's no changing him."

On the way home, I asked Mother why she hadn't told the doctor the truth; how Daddy had said the Lord had told him to take Heath off his medicine.

"I don't know," said Mother, somewhat wearily, "I guess I figured if Daddy wanted to tell him about that, he could do it himself."

"Oh," I said.

Sensing that Mother didn't want to pursue the subject any further, I let it drop. But lapsing into silence, I couldn't help but wonder about all that had happened. It appeared to me that Heath's recovery was nothing short of a miracle; and if God could work one miracle, what others might He have in store? Furthermore, if God was able to talk to Daddy as a means of communicating His way, then why couldn't He also talk to me? There seemed to be some missing link between myself and the God I prayed to. But maybe, I concluded, if I looked hard enough and waited long enough, I might eventually discover what that missing link was.

It was mid-July when our church commenced its annual summer revival, a three-day affair culminating with a Sunday evening service featuring a guest preacher. As part of the program earlier in the week, Paulette, Tim, and I were scheduled to perform as The Prewitts. Throughout, I would also be playing the piano in my usual position as church accompanist.

Having been to more revivals than I could remember, I wasn't particularly excited about this one. And by the final evening, as I walked across the road to enter the low brick building, I was downright tired. The night was muggy, and as the evening wore on, I became progressively more sleepy. By the time the preacher stepped to the pulpit, it was all I could do to keep my eyes open.

All that changed, however, less than two or three minutes into the sermon. There was something about this preacher that was different. Arresting. Perhaps it was his low-key manner and quiet speech. There was certainly nothing extraordinary about the man's delivery; he simply explained, point by point, using scriptural references as his authority, who Jesus Christ was and why He came to earth some two thousand years ago. I must have heard the same information a thousand times before, but for some reason, on this particular muggy Mississippi evening, it all seemed brand new.

For the first time I understood that Jesus was God the Father's only Son and that He humbled Himself to the human experience in order that people everywhere (including me, Cheryl!) might relate to God in an intimate way never before possible in the history of man.

For the first time, too, I understood the reason for His death on the cross—an event I had always considered tragic and horribly cruel; Jesus' death was the ultimate act of love! The reason He endured death on the cross and the horrors of Hell was because He knew that it was His Father's will that through His sacrifice people everywhere (including me,

Cheryl!) could be forgiven for their sins and given the promise of eternal life.

Finally, for the first time, I understood that it was none
other than the same Jesus Who lived and arose from the dead
some two thousand years ago, Who was alive, and real, and
working in the world today!

Enthralled, I listened as the preacher explained the two
keys to my experiencing firsthand Jesus' love, friendship, and
power: first, that I believe in Him (that is, that He wasn't a
fraud or a madman, but simply Who He said He was), and,
secondly, that I confess to Him that I am a sinner and ask
Him into my life. At first I didn't like the idea of calling myself a sinner; it sounded so harsh, as though I was a criminal
or something. But then, as if to answer my question, the
preacher explained that everyone is a sinner—that is, no matter how hard people try, they are incapable of being as good
as they want or know they should be.

It was all too much. For the first time I fully understood,
in a totally new way, what it meant to be a Christian. Moreover, whether or not I was to become one was a decision, I
realized, that could only be made by me. To take that step
would mean that it would then be my duty (and privilege!)
to discover for what reason God had put me into the world.
And once that purpose had been discovered, it would then be
my duty to pursue that path the very best I could. To become a Christian meant so many things. . . . But throughout, I would never be alone. I would always have Jesus as my
very real friend and guide. I would always have Jesus to talk
to God the Father through, and to follow as an example.

"For God so loved the world, that he gave his only begotten
Son, that whosoever believeth in him should not perish, but have
everlasting life" (John 3:16).

Upon hearing the preacher's closing words and invitation
to accept Christ, my heart pounded wildly. For a moment I

hesitated, but then, bursting into tears, I ran down the aisle and fell to my knees at the altar rail. I had no doubts. I had no fears. More than anything else in the world, I wanted Jesus to come into my life. *Jesus, I was certain, was my missing link to God.*

"Lord Jesus," I prayed, "thank You for dying on the cross for my sins. Thank You for the gift of eternal life. Oh, Jesus, I need You so much! Come into my life—come into my heart. Live in me, Lord, and make me the person You want me to be. Thank You, Jesus. Amen."

Later, after returning to my seat, I found myself vaguely wondering what some of the folks in the congregation must have thought upon seeing me up at the altar. After all, most of my life had been spent in churches, playing and singing gospel music. Hadn't I always been a believer? But no, it was clear to me I hadn't. And even now, just moments after becoming one, it was difficult to explain exactly how I had changed—I only knew that I was different. Like a new person. And with my new friend, Jesus, I felt as though I were on the threshold of a very big adventure.

Walking across the road toward home, I felt Daddy come up from behind me and put his arm around my shoulders.

"Honey," he said, "I was mighty glad to see what you did tonight. Mighty glad."

"You were?" I asked.

"Yep," he replied. "I had a feeling something like this was going to happen. Tell you what. Tonight, when we have our Bible reading, I'm gonna ask you to read. It's just a short little passage—but I think it's one the Lord's intended for you."

"For me?" I asked. For some reason, the idea of the Lord having a personal message for me didn't seem at all as unlikely as it had in the past. And to hear Daddy speak in that manner no longer made me feel uncomfortable—but rather excited.

"That's right," said Daddy. "I'll see you later." With that, he loped across the road to join Mother, who was already at the front door.

Later that evening, as we gathered in the music room, I could hardly wait for Daddy to announce the scripture we would be reading and talking about. As I thumbed through the pages of my Bible, it was as though I were holding in my hands all the wisdom of the ages, the answers to any and every question. I'd never regarded the Bible in that way before—as something so relevant to my life, so—personal. For the first time I began to understand the meaning behind one of Daddy's favorite expressions: "There's power in the Word."

Once everyone had assembled, Daddy opened his Bible and placed his broad hand, palm down, on the open pages.

"Tonight," he said, "we're going to read a fairly short verse; in fact, it's barely one sentence long. Must admit, too, it's a verse not too popular with lots of folks. I'm talking about Matthew 5:48."

There was silence in the room, save for the flutter of pages as we turned to the passage.

Glancing at the verse, I felt myself wince. It was hardly the message of personal encouragement that I had been hoping for. How could Daddy have thought it was meant for me?

"Cheryl?" Daddy said, "Would you read for us, please?"

Trying not to show my disappointment, I read the verse — Jesus' words to His disciples — aloud: ''You, therefore, must be perfect, as your heavenly Father is perfect (paraphrased).''

"*Perfect?*" echoed Tim, skeptically.

"But nobody's perfect," said Paulette.

"How, Hosea?" asked Mother. "It's not possible, is it?"

"Like I said," repeated Daddy, "this is a hard passage. Lots of folks don't like it. But what I think Jesus is saying is that He wants us to *try*. He, you see, is perfect, and if we just put forth the effort, He promises to help us. That's what makes life as a Christian so exciting; it's a continual process of being transformed into a new and better person, while at the same time growing closer to God."

"Oh," said Mother.

Not much more was said about the passage; it seemed to have affected the others in much the same way it had me. After saying a closing prayer, everyone got up to go to bed.

"Coming?" asked Mother, who, after picking up Heath's toys and stashing them in the corner, was the last to leave.

"Soon," I replied. Determined to find some deeper, more personal meaning out of the evening's reading, I wanted to sit a while longer and think about it.

"Well then," said Mother, "good night." She bent down and kissed the top of my head. "Turn out the light when you're done, all right?"

"Right," I said.

Opening my Bible, I turned again to Matthew 5:48 and reread the passage: "You, therefore, must be perfect, as your heavenly Father is perfect."

Perfect?

I recalled Tim's skepticism at the idea. *True*, I thought, *to be perfect did seem to be an impossibility. On the other hand, it was also true that with God's help, anything was possible. So what if, I wondered, what if, with God's help, it was possible to become perfect—or at least try? What, then, might be some areas in my life that could use some improvement?*

With that, I almost laughed out loud.

As a musician, I might have been tops at Weir School, but in the eyes of the world, I was nothing more than a novice.

As a gospel performer, too, I was merely one of many in

the ranks of backwoods amateurs; it would be a long, long time before The Prewitts would ever be rubbing shoulders with the likes of The Blackwood Brothers.

And as far as my looks were concerned—at this, I had to laugh. With a mouth crowded with crooked teeth, a face tracked with scars, and two legs of unequal length, I was hardly an all-American beauty!

Clearly, I concluded, my situation was hopeless. The only way I could even begin to approach perfection in any area of my life would be to turn myself in for a complete overhaul.

Suddenly, I was struck with the impression that this—to turn myself in—might very well be exactly what Jesus wanted me to do! And the more I thought about it, the more sense it made. Daddy was right! This scripture had been for me!

Having asked Jesus to enter and take control of my life, He was, in turn, requesting of me a total make-over. An all-new improved Cheryl. "You're not a little girl anymore," He seemed to be saying. "You belong to Me now, and it's time you grew up."

This time, however, the prospect of growing up no longer was frightening. With Jesus as my friend and guide, there seemed to be an inherent purpose and bright promise to the future. "Focus on the positive," He seemed to be telling me. "Keep on trying. Keep on smiling."

It all made perfect sense.

True, I thought, I may not be the best pianist in the world, but I could keep on practicing. And true, The Prewitts may not be the best-known gospel group in the south—or in Choctaw County, for that matter—but there was nothing to stop us from trying. And true, I may not be the prettiest girl at Weir School—but who said I couldn't make the most of what I had? I could conceal my scars with makeup. I could work on being beautiful on the inside. I could hope, in the end, that folks would remember me not for my crooked teeth, but for my smile.

Perfect?

I closed my Bible and turned out the light.

If perfect was what Jesus wanted me to be, then the least I could do was try.

"HEATH, BABY," I said, "come here a minute. Do you
think you know 'Operator' well enough to sing it tonight?"

"Sure," he replied, setting down his microphone and coming over to join me at the piano. "I know I can."

We were taking a break from an evening performance as
"The Prewitts" at a local church. Before breaking, we had
asked for requests for the second half of the show. One
member of the congregation had asked that we sing "Operator," an upbeat contemporary gospel song that compares
speaking to God in prayer with making a long-distance telephone call. We'd worked long hours on the number at home,
but hadn't yet performed it in public. Heath, six years old
now and nearly fully recovered from the accident, had been
performing with us for the past year and sang the featured
part.

"Let's run through it once, okay?" I suggested.

"Okay," he replied, plopping himself down next to me on
the piano bench.

It was spring, 1973, and our family gospel group had
changed a lot over the past few years—not only in size, but in
the types of songs we sang and in the Christian witness we
shared between numbers.

Musically, we were moving away from solely traditional
gospel programs that consisted only of classics such as
"Amazing Grace" and "How Great Thou Art"—though
being guaranteed crowd-pleasers, such songs were always included. More and more we found ourselves experimenting
with the more contemporary sounds in gospel music—songs
like "Operator," which incorporated a pop-rock beat and included instruments other than the piano and tambourine.
Tim was learning to play the bass guitar, and it was our hope
to eventually add some other members to the group who
would play flute and drums. At first Daddy had balked when

confronted with such changes, but after hearing us perform some of the new songs and studying their lyrics, he had been quickly convinced of their merit. As always, Daddy's primary concern was that the music we sang would ultimately serve to communicate some aspect of the gospel. Viewing our group as a genuine ministry, he was always willing to try new methods that might do the job more effectively; the contemporary gospel sound, he felt, might better reach young people and others who, for one reason or another, didn't care for traditional gospel music.

An even more dramatic change had been our increasing boldness in speaking out about God's love and miracle-working power as we had experienced it in our lives. While each member of the group was, during the course of a performance, given the opportunity to share his or her personal testimony, it seemed that in recent years I had come to be the main spokesperson for the group. Nothing made me happier or more excited than telling people about the Lord; nearly every program found me sharing with the audience the honest-to-goodness miracles He had worked in our own family—Heath's recovery and my learning to walk again. Sometimes when I got to speaking about God's love, it was as though I was filled to overflowing with His Spirit, and the words came spilling out. Basically, my message was this: "Not only is God able to love you, but He *wants* to love you. He loves you and cares for you, and He has a wonderful plan for your life—but it's up to you to accept Him. There now," I'd conclude, "I've told you all I know, and now the decision is left to you. I only hope you give God a chance to show how much He loves you." Often we closed our programs with an invitation for people to accept Christ. Many did.

Turning to Heath, I was just about to join him in going over the lyrics to "Operator," when we were interrupted by the sound of the preacher's voice over Heath's unattended microphone. His face was flushed and his movements agitated as he cleared his throat and began to speak.

"I'm sorry, folks," he said to the congregation, "but the evening is over. I apologize for what you've just seen and heard. Please be assured that it won't happen again."

Stunned, I pulled Heath close to me as though to protect him from the suddenly ugly atmosphere.

"And as for you-all," the preacher continued, casting his eyes around the room to include all of us—including Mother and Daddy, who were sitting in the front row—"I'm sorry for you, too. I'm sorry I ever asked you to come here. You are no longer welcome in this church. I must ask you to leave."

"Now hold on here," Daddy stood to protest.

"I'm sorry," repeated the preacher. "But I don't like your music. And I don't like what your youngsters have to say. Now if you'll excuse me, please, there are some members of my congregation that I've got some explaining to do to."

"Come on, Heath," I said in a low voice, blinking furiously to hold back tears, "let's go." Gathering our music, I closed the lid over the piano. Taking Heath by the hand, I walked with him out to the car.

No one said a word as we loaded the trunk with our sound equipment and instruments. As we headed home, the heavy silence was broken only by my increasingly loud sniffs.

Suddenly, Daddy pulled over to the side of the road and stopped the car.

"Now what," he asked, fixing his eyes on me in the rear view mirror, "is all this fuss about? Tell me. Tell me all about it."

"But Daddy," I sobbed, amazed at his apparent calm in spite of what had happened at the church. "They didn't like us. They told us to go. They don't ever want us to come back. Oh, Daddy, what did we do wrong?"

"You kids didn't do anything wrong," replied Daddy.

"Some folks just can't tolerate music other than what they're used to hearing. And other folks—including some preachers—don't like hearing talk about a God that's loving and still works miracles. It makes 'em nervous.

"Cheryl, honey," Daddy turned around to face me, "you know what's right, don't you? You know what's true. Now what you told those folks tonight about God—such things are what you know to be right and true, correct?"

"Yes," I replied.

"Well then," he said, as if the matter was settled.

"But Daddy," I countered, "what if it happens again?"

"So it happens," he said. "And sure as my name is Hosea Prewitt, it will."

Daddy, unfortunately, was right. This wasn't the first time a church, or preacher, had been less than happy with what we had to say and sing. Though most folks in the area loved our performances, there were always a few who didn't. Still, whenever it happened, the experience continued to cause me deep distress.

"Now I don't want anyone brooding over this," Daddy said, as he steered the car back on the road and continued home. "As far as your music goes, it's just a matter of time; new things take getting used to. Folks will come around. But as far as the way some choose to underestimate our Lord—well, that's something that may never change. Nothing we can do about it. Specially worry."

Still, I was concerned for our group.

Musically, I knew that we were very good, and often I felt we were on the verge of something big. Most of our bookings, however, stemmed from word-of-mouth recommendations; often I felt there must be better, more sophisticated means of promoting ourselves—though I didn't know how to go about discovering them. More than once I had a sneaky suspicion that when it came to techniques of publicity and promotion, The Prewitts were lost somewhere in the Stone Age.

One night, as we were about to begin a rehearsal at home, I mentioned the matter to Paulette, Tim, and Heath, who all agreed it was something worth praying about. Soon after, however, the subject was dropped—forgotten for the moment in the more immediate concerns of the evening such as finding the whereabouts of Paulette's tambourine and Heath's pet frog.

On the third Sunday in May, our church held its annual Memorial Day Homecoming service, a daylong event that featured an out-of-town guest speaker and potluck dinner on the grounds.

That morning at breakfast, Tim punched me on the arm and said, teasingly, "You better play the piano real good today, Cheryl, 'cause a Blackwood's gonna be there listening."

"What?" I asked, my interest in the name Blackwood overriding my annoyance at Tim. "What are you talking about, Tim Prewitt? And don't talk with your mouth full."

"Doyle Blackwood," replied Tim, deliberately smacking his lips. "Doyle Blackwood's come to town to be our guest speaker for Memorial Sunday."

"Really?" I asked, turning to Daddy. "Daddy, is what Tim says true?"

"Yep," he replied. "I heard the man's good, too."

Doyle Blackwood, one of the original members of The Blackwood Brothers, was like a legend to me. Though he no longer sang with the group (preferring life at home at his small farm in Memphis, with his wife, Lavez, and children, Terry and Kay, to the grueling life on the road), he still made frequent public appearances throughout the South—sometimes joining his brothers, but more often alone. Most of the time he managed a small record and book shop in

Memphis; every once in a while he returned to Ackerman to visit kin and his parents' old homestead.

Though I'd heard a lot about Doyle Blackwood, I'd never met him, and the thought of seeing him in less than an hour's time made me so excited I could hardly finish my breakfast.

Once at church and seated at the piano, I searched the congregation for a glimpse of the man—a futile effort, as I had no idea what he looked like. Suddenly, I caught sight of Tim, who was pointing with all his might toward the right-hand side of the altar area where our guest speakers usually sat. There, chatting softly with our preacher, was Doyle Blackwood.

At first I was startled at his appearance; standing only five foot three and certainly weighing not much more than me, he reminded me for all the world of a little red squirrel. His bespectacled brown eyes were bright and curious, his manner alert, and movements spry.

But all that was forgotten the moment he began to sing, overshadowed by the sheer beauty of his pure, tremulous tenor and by the genuine love he communicated for both his audience and for the Lord.

His preaching was equally spellbinding; with verve more suited to someone half his age, he spoke about the fact that as Christians, we "live in a body, have a mind, but are—in essence—spirit." Being such a little bitty person, and fairly exploding with vitality, he was his own best witness. "Sometimes," he joked, "I've got to watch out when I get to thinking that my body's as big as my spirit. A man could get hurt that way."

Later on in the service, Paulette, Tim, Heath, and I sang. I wasn't sure if it was my imagination, but I thought Doyle seemed particularly enthused over our performance; his hearty "A-men!" at its close was enough to extinguish the altar candles. Afterward, when the service had ended and everyone was heading outside to set up the tables for Sunday dinner, I summoned all my nerve and walked up to Doyle, who was just finishing a conversation with another member of the congregation.

"Howdy, Mr. Blackwood," I said, giving him a great big hug. "My name's Cheryl Prewitt, and I think you're great."

"Well I think you're pretty great yourself," he replied, returning my hug. "But please call me Doyle. You know, young lady, I was watching you up there playing that old piano today—not bad." His eyes twinkled with enthusiasm.

"Oh, Mr. Blackwood," I said excitedly, "thank you! Thank you so much! Did you meet my family yet? I'd love for you to meet my family."

"Well, I'd like that very much," he replied. "Mind if I join y'all for dinner?"

"Mind?" I cried. "Oh, Mr. Blackwood, that would be wonderful! I'll save you a seat."

Squeezing his hand, I ran off to join Mother and Daddy and tell them about our conversation.

Thus began a relationship the likes of which I'd never known; in ensuing weeks, Doyle Blackwood and I grew to be the best of friends. To casual observers, we must have been an odd couple to be sure—we were, however, kindred spirits.

A few weeks after our first meeting, Doyle called me to let me know that he and his wife, Lavez, were heading down our way from Memphis and were wondering if I might want to join them for a Sunday drive. When Mother and Daddy agreed to let me go, I thought I might expire on the spot.

It was a sunny summer afternoon, and after stopping first to visit with Doyle's older sister, Lena Cain, we headed for the old Blackwood homestead and nearby cemetery where Doyle's parents were buried. We'd paid our respects and reminisced for maybe half an hour or so, when Doyle announced that he'd very much like to spend the rest of the day hunting for petrified wood.

Lavez apparently had quite a rock garden at their Memphis

home, and there was nothing Doyle enjoyed more than adding to her already extensive collection. No one knew for certain which came first—Lavez's garden or Doyle's hobby. At any rate, to take off into the piny woods in search of petrified wood (or "hickory rocks," as Doyle preferred to call those most elusive of all stones) was his favorite pastime.

One of Lavez's favorite stories was about the time she and Doyle went out for a drive one overcast afternoon, and Doyle insisted that they stop the car to hunt for some rocks.

"But I don't want to go rock hunting," protested Lavez. "It looks like rain."

"Well, I do," replied Doyle stubbornly, pulling over to the side of the road and parking the car. "This looks like especially good rock country. With a little luck, I might even find some hickory rocks." With a wave of his hand, he disappeared into the woods.

When more than an hour had passed and Doyle still hadn't returned, Lavez began to worry. Adding to her concern, the skies opened, and it poured buckets. When the cloudburst had ended, Lavez peered into the woods, hoping for a sign—any sign—of Doyle. Much to her relief, off in the distance, she saw his small rain-soaked figure approaching the car. Suspenders drooping, he was, as usual, returning from his rock hunt empty-handed.

"What I want to know," he said disgustedly, as he leaned against Lavez's open car door and poured water out of his boots, "is why you didn't blow the horn."

"Why didn't I blow the horn?" cried Lavez, trying not to laugh. "How was I to know you were lost?"

Other times, when Doyle and I were alone, we'd spend hours talking about spiritual things: a Bible verse, a character in the Old Testament, and—Doyle's favorite subject—what it meant to live in the world as a Christian today. When it came to Christianity, Doyle had all the enthusiasm and joy of a new convert; well into his sixties, however, he also possessed

the wisdom gained through a lifetime that had not been without hardship and struggles. Throughout, he had the most
impish sense of humor; nothing escaped his childlike curios-
ity. And he was always calling or writing me letters. Once,
while attending a convention in Tulsa, Oklahoma, he impulsively clipped and mailed me a newspaper photo of a tremendously fat man cooling off in a swimming pool. Another
time, while on a flight from Chattanooga to Memphis, he
dashed me a note on airline stationery, making sure to also
enclose the salt and pepper containers from his in-flight dinner. Funny and loving as Doyle could be, he was, primarily—
all hundred and six pounds of him—every ounce a musician.

From the start, Doyle had expressed excitement about our
family's group. On the afternoon of our first meeting, I overheard him asking Daddy about our current bookings and
how we went about promoting ourselves. Thoroughly acquainted with the gospel music scene—from grass-roots stir-
rings on up to the Grand Ole Opry—he suggested that we
try our luck performing in places other than churches, such
as county and state fairs. In addition, he secured some appearances for us at churches in and around Memphis and
offered us some much-needed pointers about promotion techniques such as sending out news releases with black and
white glossy photos of our group to local papers prior to our
appearances. Often he traveled miles out of his way to introduce us, more than once as the final act about to go on at
midnight under a rain-soaked tent at some county fair. I
guess the most exciting moment occurred when Doyle encouraged us to record a third album as The Prewitts (years
earlier, we had recorded two others at considerable expense
and with little public response) for which he wanted to write
the back-jacket introduction. It was all very thrilling;
Doyle's influence lent to The Prewitts the touch of profes-
sionalism that had for so long been needed.

Musically, he encouraged us to continue offering audiences

a blend of traditional and contemporary gospel sounds as we had been doing. Even more strongly, he encouraged us to continue speaking out boldly about the Lord. Like Daddy, Doyle considered our performances to be ministerial first and entertaining second. Also like Daddy, he felt it of utmost importance that our private lives be as much a witness as our publicly professed faith.

As months passed and our popularity grew, more and more it seemed that the two—our personal lives and our public identity as Christians—became inextricably entwined. For me, this became an increasing source of conflict which, by the end of eleventh grade, reached crisis proportions.

My junior year had been busy to a degree I'd never before experienced. At home, I had my hands full with up to fifty private piano students (at Becky's urging I had begun to teach in the ninth grade), homework, rehearsals with the family, and—most every weekend—performances that took us out of town.

At school, my schedule was no less hectic. Having integrated in 1970, Weir School had nearly doubled in size; competition was stiff, and good grades harder to come by. Still, I managed to maintain a 3.5 to 4.0 average and was a member of Beta Club, Weir High's honor society. With Becky, I continued to take lessons (piano and voice), sing with the Girls' Sextet, coach the Boys' Quartet, and accompany the other choral groups. I also continued to compete in state recitals and in tenth grade accepted a paying position to teach basic music instruction to elementary students in a nearby county. In addition, I also sang, played, and arranged for The Young and Tender, a pop group including Angela, myself, Sue Cutts (Mr. DeWitt Cutts's daughter), and Ralph Gordon (a friend who played drums), which styled itself after The Carpenters. Such activities, too, often called for out-of-town performances.

I guess I was popular enough; that is, I had a lot of friends and was an involved student. But at some point I became aware that there was a whole social scene taking place after school hours of which I was decidedly not a part. While I often told myself the reason I was excluded was because I was simply not available, deep down inside I knew that was not true. More than once I had received invitations and turned them down. This was because lots of the parties included drinking, smoking, and—for those so inclined—sex. Sometimes the boys called me "preacher girl," and though I knew they were only kidding (many were good friends), it hurt.

If only they knew, I often thought, *how badly I wanted to be included—to be like them, to drink and party—or at least give it a try*. While my innermost being said no (not only because I had a Christian reputation to maintain, but because I couldn't bear the thought of disappointing people like Doyle), I still flirted with danger by picking up boyfriends at out of town Beta Club conventions and state choral competitions. Such relationships were admittedly phony, nothing more than big talk and empty promises made within the security of knowing that in twenty-four hours I'd be safely home.

As the year progressed, the battle being waged inside me grew increasingly more fierce. Frustrated with my goody-goody image, I desperately wanted to date and go to parties. And if I liked a boy, I wanted to be free to express my affection with hugs and kisses. But it was all so confusing. How much was too much? And what if my behavior was misinterpreted? (Frequently I recalled the incident with the man in our store that had taken place three years earlier.)

Still, the more I thought about it, the more dissatisfied I became with my lot as a gospel-singing Christian. Sometimes when performing with my family on a Friday or Saturday night, I found myself dreaming enviously about what my school friends were up to. Here I was in church, while they were out having fun.

In early May, a friend who was a grade ahead of me asked me to the senior party which was to take place at the end of the month. Though he was a nice enough fellow and I knew him pretty well, I declined. The senior party had a bit of a bad reputation; often held at some secluded woodsy place, there was sure to be lots of drinking, smoking, and general wild times. My friend, however, must have detected a note of wistfulness to my refusal; a week later he called and asked me again. This time, swallowing hard, I said yes—with the understanding that if there was a lot of bad stuff going on, we wouldn't stay.

My friend agreed, and we set the time that he would pick me up.

The party was on a Friday night. Early that afternoon, I received a phone call from Doyle.

"You free tonight?" he asked. "I'm singing at a church not too far from your place, and I thought you might want to be my accompanist."

"Oh, Doyle," I replied, "I'd love to, but I can't. I've—uh, got a date."

"Too bad," said Doyle. "I'll miss you." He paused. "Where you going, anyhow?"

"Oh," I said lamely, "nowhere special. Just a party. Kids from school."

"I see," said Doyle, a note of surprise in his voice. "Well, be good. Guess I'll be seeing you all next weekend down at Wood Springs, right?"

"Right," I said, suddenly very anxious for our conversation to be ended. "See you then."

Wood Springs was a community some nine miles north of us. One of the churches there had scheduled both Doyle and our family to perform for their revival the following weekend.

As I hung up the phone and went upstairs to prepare for my date, I wondered what Doyle had been like at my age; if he, as a young Christian, had ever felt torn between wanting to be accepted by the other kids and wanting to do what was right.

Such thoughts disappeared, however, as with mounting excitement I began to anticipate the evening ahead. Carefully I selected my perfume, applied my mascara, dotted my cheeks with rouge. Ready to go nearly an hour before my date was supposed to pick me up, I giggled delightedly in making him wait a full five minutes before I greeted him downstairs. His approving glance as I entered the room made my pulse quicken. As he walked me to the car and closed my door, I could hardly wait to get to the party.

It was a steamy night. For the first few minutes I chattered gaily as we drove. After a while, lapsing into silence, I watched as the car lights picked out the curves in the dirt road ahead.

"Where are we going, anyhow?" I asked.

"The old schoolhouse," my friend replied. "Down near Choctaw Lake."

"The old schoolhouse?" I said. "But that's in the middle of nowhere."

"That's right," my friend said, taking hold of my hand. "Now don't you get yourself all worked up, Cheryl. Everything's gonna be just fine." Then, removing his hand from mine, he pointed toward a lighted area of woods in the distance. "Look," he said. "Up ahead. That's where we're going."

Pulling off to the side of the road, we joined the string of parked cars that led to the party. As we approached the clearing where the party was in full swing, I felt my heart sink.

Headlights illuminated the thickly wooded area in garish relief, their harsh glare revealing silhouette forms of embracing couples leaning against the trees and along the side of the old schoolhouse. Shadowy figures could also be seen moving within the ramshackle building, where candles flickered and tinny music blared from someone's transistor radio. Heavy with the smell of beer and cigarette smoke, the atmosphere was that of a brewing storm; sporadic outbursts of laughter like threatening thundercracks.

The party was everything I had imagined—but far from exciting, it seemed menacing—and wrong. Overwhelmed with a sense of not belonging, I desperately wanted to leave.

Recalling the condition under which I had accepted the date, I mentioned my uneasiness to my friend and asked him to take me home.

"Soon," he replied. "But first I've got some friends I want to talk to."

"All right," I said. "I'll meet you back at the car."

Fifteen minutes had passed when finally my friend returned.

"Sorry you're not having more fun," he said, "—preacher girl." He laughed. "I'm sorry," he added, as I cast him a dismayed look. "Just kidding." He turned on the engine. "Let's go."

As we drove off into the darkness, however, I felt more regret than relief at our decision to leave the party. Already the old struggle was returning inside me. Once again, I'd lived up to my reputation as a good little girl. Once again, I'd passed up an opportunity to let loose and have fun.

Suddenly, I noticed that we were headed in a direction opposite that from which we had come. I also noticed the distinct odor of whiskey on my friend's breath.

"Hey," I said, "what were you doing back there with your friends? And where are you taking me?"

"Now just sit tight," he replied. "We're going for a little ride, that's all."

"I don't want to go for a ride," I said. "I want to go home."

"Oh, I think this is one ride you'll like," he said. "We're going down to Choctaw Lake. You like the lake, don't you?"

I said nothing.

Up ahead, I could see the black glassy surface of the moonlit lake, the ring of cars surrounding its sandy shore. Choctaw Lake was the area's hottest parking spot. I couldn't believe I was there. While frightening, it was at the same time thrilling. *Now was my chance*, I thought, *maybe my last chance, to have some fun.*

My heart was pounding as my friend guided the car to a secluded area, parked, and turned off the engine. But the moment I felt him lunge toward me, all my excitement drained and was replaced by cold, raw fear.

"What are you doing?" I cried.

But it was too late.

Before I knew what was happening, he was all over me, breathing heavily and kissing me on the lips. Struggling with all my might, with one hand I managed to reach behind me and grab hold of the door latch. Opening the door, I threw myself out onto the firm ground—leaving my friend, confused and angry, sprawled across the front seat.

"You touch me again, and I'll scream!" I yelled. "I'll scream till the police come! And I can scream good, you know! I can scream real good!"

"Aw, c'mon, Cheryl," my friend pleaded miserably. "I'm sorry. Please don't scream. I thought you *wanted* to come here. I thought that's what you had in mind from the start."

"What?" I cried, in my most offended tone. "Are you saying I asked for this kind of treatment? What kind of a person do you think I am?"

"Aw, c'mon, Cheryl," my friend repeated. "I said I'm sorry. What more do you want? Get back in the car, and I'll take you home."

As we drove along in stony silence, I thought about my friend's accusation—that I had asked for the evening he had offered me—and with a pang of guilt, I realized that he was right. Sick with shame, I began to worry about possible repercussions from the incident. What if my friend had a big mouth and told all the other guys at school about our time together? Worse—and I cringed at the thought—what would someone like Doyle think, if he ever found out?

Once home, my friend insisted on escorting me to the front door; both of us, I think, didn't want the evening to end on an entirely sour note.

"Well," I said lightly, as I reached for his hand and stepped to the pavement. "I'd say this is the last time you'll ever see me in this car."

"I'd say you're right," he replied with a rueful smile.

Together, in silence, we walked to the front door.

"Good night, Cheryl," he said, as he opened the door for me. "Take care of yourself."

That night, as I lay awake in bed, I once again was confronted with the problem of my conflicting desires. If nothing else, the evening has served to clearly point out that I couldn't continue to straddle the fence much longer before getting myself into far more serious situations than having to fend off the advances of a semi-intoxicated friend on the shores of Choctaw Lake. Acutely aware of my hypocrisy, for the first time I understood what the apostle Paul was suffering when he wrote, "I do not understand my own actions. For I do not do what I want, but I do the very thing I hate" (Romans 7:15 paraphrased), and the wisdom of James when he wrote of the woes suffered by the "double-minded man . . . unstable in all his ways." (James 1:7-8)

"Father," I prayed before going to sleep, "You know I've got a real thorny problem here; deep down inside, I want to do what's right, but there's this other part of me that won't cooperate. I want to be Yours, Father—one hundred percent

Yours. Please give me a sign, some sort of example to follow, that will help me overcome this problem area in my life. In Jesus' name I pray. Amen."

The week that followed was more or less uneventful. Frequently I bumped into my friend in the hallways at school. Our exchanges, however, were polite and not uncomfortable. Much to my relief, it was evident that the episode at Choctaw Lake would remain our own little secret.

On Saturday I joined my family and headed up to Wood Springs to meet up with Doyle and perform at the church revival.

That evening, as I listened to Doyle sing and preach, it occurred to me that for the first time in a long time I was not spending the evening in a state of discontent, wondering what my friends were up to. Instead, I was fascinated by what a genuinely good time Doyle seemed to be having. Recalling our times together, I was struck with the realization that Doyle *always* seemed to have a good time—whether hunting for hickory rocks or singing his heart out in a church on a Saturday night. Here, clearly, was a man who had a definite sense of what was right and a corresponding desire to do it. Here was a single-minded man, for whom the Christian faith was not a deterrent but a means to having fun!

When the service had ended, Doyle came over to where Heath and I were gathering our music and equipment in preparation for the return trip home.

"You've been looking mighty thoughtful this evening, young lady," he said. "How'd you and your brother like a lift home with me? That way, the three of us can have a good visit."

"Sure," I said. "Sounds good to me." I turned to Heath. "Want to ride home with Doyle?"

"Yeah!" exclaimed Heath. "That'd be neat!"

Doyle drove a little red pick-up truck, his trademark, which Heath absolutely loved to ride in. Because he was so tiny, Doyle sat on a small round cushion that elevated him a good three inches.

"Tell me," said Doyle, as we hopped in the truck and began to follow the others home, "what's been on your mind lately? What's the Lord been doing in your life?"

For a moment I said nothing—both embarrassed at the nature of my recent dilemma and fearful of Doyle's disappointment in me lest I tell him. But suddenly it seemed that I could hold it in no longer, and in a torrent of words I spilled out my story—all about my running battle with wanting to be like the other kids, yet wanting to be good, and, ultimately, about the incident at Choctaw Lake.

Doyle listened carefully. And when I had finished, he was quiet for quite some time. Finally, he spoke.

"Well, honey," he said thoughtfully, "when I was a young man, just about your age, I suffered exactly the same problem. But at some point I came to the conclusion that there's no way possible to mix the two worlds—the world of human nature and the world of the spirit—and have it all come out rosy. It's all or nothing; you're either in the boat or out. There comes a time when you've simply got to make a decision where you want to stand—and it's a decision that only you can make. But I'll promise you this: once you make your decision to follow God's way—and really mean it—you can be sure the Lord will help you all the way." He paused. "Now I don't know, Cheryl, if that helps you any, but—"

"Oh, Doyle," I cried, my heart nearly bursting with love, "you'll never know how much you've helped me—not only by what you've said, but by just being you!"

Impulsively, I reached across the seat, threw my arms around his tiny body, and hugged him with all my might.

"Well, hallelujah!" grinned Doyle. "Praise the Lord!"

SEATED IN Dr. Snead's office, I gazed at the assorted wood carvings and knickknacks that crowded his desk. It was July 1974, the summer before my senior year, and I was waiting for him to join me for the little chat we typically had after each of my visits. I'd been seeing Dr. Snead for back treatments for over six years now, and in the course of that time the two of us had become close friends.

Now, I grinned as he entered the room, my file in his hand.

"Well, Cheryl," he said, easing himself into the swivel chair behind his desk, "you must be feeling pretty good. That back of yours is a far piece improved from what it was a few years ago."

Though Dr. Snead's voice was cheerful enough, his manner was tense—not that at all of an old friend sharing good news. His troubled eyes brought back memories of my old visits with doctors—recollections of hospitals and pain and gloomy prognoses. I felt a sinking sensation in my stomach.

"Your back is better," he went on, "but I'm afraid there may be a potential problem with your leg."

"Problem?" My voice rose in alarm. "How can there be a problem? My leg is healed. My leg is *fine*." My head felt all cottony and light. True, my left leg was still short, but it was a small handicap—no big deal. Though I still limped and Mother continued to hem my clothes, most folks didn't even know about my leg. Not even some of my closest friends. "What kind of problem?" I asked.

"It's nothing to worry about today," said Dr. Snead, "but it's bound to affect you in the future"—he paused—"if you ever decide you want to have a family."

"What do you mean?" I asked. "What are you talking about?"

"I'm sorry," he replied, "but because of the way your old

injury has mended—the way your shortened leg has affected the alignment of your hips—it's highly unlikely that you'll ever be able to have children. It's something that can't be fixed. I mean, we can't make your leg longer."

"Oh," I said dully.

At first, the full meaning of Dr. Snead's words didn't sink in. Motherhood was an issue that seemed a million years away. Still, I guess I'd always considered it to be a likely eventuality in my life. To suddenly have no choice in the matter was difficult to absorb.

"Are you all right?" asked Dr. Snead.

"Fine," I said quietly. I reached to the floor for my pocketbook. Slowly, I stood up. "I think I want to go home now."

Mother was waiting for me when I got home. Getting supper ready, she was standing over the kitchen counter.

"How'd it go?" she asked, pushing aside a half-filled pot of peeled potatoes. "Feel better?"

I opened my mouth to answer, but the words didn't come. I burst into tears.

"*Cheryl*," cried Mother, rushing to my side, "what is it?"

Stricken, she listened as I told her what Dr. Snead had said. She held me tightly. Then she led me over to the kitchen table, sat me down, and pulled another chair around to sit next to me.

"Honey," she said, "there's only one thing we can do in a situation like this: we've just got to hand this problem over to the Lord. He's the only One Who can help. He's done it before, you know. He'll do it again."

Mother's words were comforting, encouraging, and in my heart I knew they held the truth. Jesus was listening. He was ready and waiting to answer our prayers if—and here was the key—if only I believed. I'd believed when I was eleven and learned to walk again. I'd believed when I was fourteen and became a Christian. Why, then, was it so difficult for me to believe today?

"Mother?" I said quietly.

"Yes?"

"Pray for me," I said. "Pray that I have the faith to believe that Jesus can heal me."

"Of course I will," said Mother. "We all will. This is a mighty tough problem—but there's nothing too tough for our Lord. Now dry your eyes and get ready for supper. We'll talk more about this later. Madelyn and Web Wood are stopping by tonight, you know; they're bringing a young couple with them who want to record a gospel album. Madelyn thought we might be able to offer them some pointers."

"Oh, Mother," I said, "do I have to be there? I really don't feel like it."

"I think it would be nice," said Mother. "Especially when you consider all Madelyn's people have done for us."

"All right," I agreed reluctantly.

Madelyn Wood was Doyle Blackwood's niece—his older sister, Lena Cain's, daughter. Like most Blackwoods, Madelyn was tremendously gifted musically. An accomplished pianist, for years she had been the area's most sought after music teacher. She had, in fact, been the woman who had taught Becky when she was a young girl. I had first met Madelyn a few years earlier while rehearsing with the Girls' Sextet at Becky's house. (Sometimes Becky asked Madelyn to join us to lend her expert ear.) In recent months I'd also started to teach piano to her son, Sammy, and through this relationship was beginning to feel as though I knew her well. Besides, it seemed that both Becky and Doyle couldn't say enough good about the woman; in addition to her wide renown as a top musician, she was equally well known for her unusually strong faith.

By the time Madelyn and the others arrived that evening, I was feeling a bit more sociable; only occasionally did fleeting recollections of my visit with Dr. Snead interfere with my enjoyment of the occasion. Those feelings must have shown, however; after we'd finished singing and talking shop and were relaxing with coffee and fresh-baked cinnamon bread, I noticed Madelyn in a far corner of the music room speaking privately with Mother. Both wore concerned expressions and every once in a while they glanced toward my direction. Finally, unable to stand it any longer, I left my seat and approached them.

"Now what all is going on here?" I asked with a grin. "I have a distinct feeling that you-all are talking about me and I'd like very much to know what about."

Madelyn, never one to sidestep an issue, was quick to answer.

"You seemed a little low tonight, Cheryl, so I asked your mother what the trouble was. She told me about your leg—how it healed short and how Sam Snead says you might have a problem when it comes to having kids. I never knew about your leg, Cheryl. All this comes as a real surprise to me."

"Well, I guess I hide it pretty well," I said. "Besides, it's really nothing."

"Nothing?" cried Madelyn, her green eyes blazing. For a little lady, she—like Doyle—had a lot of spunk. "You call a short leg nothing? I'd say it's something—something that should be taken care of, and as soon as possible."

"But Madelyn," I protested, "there's really nothing that can be done. The doctors say—"

"Cheryl, darlin'," Madelyn interrupted, "I'm not talking about what doctors say. Now before we carry this discussion further, I'd like to see that leg of yours. That is, if it's all right with you."

"Sure," I replied. "Why not? But really, Madelyn, there's nothing that can be done—"

"Now you just hush with all that negative talk," said Madelyn, "and show me your leg."

By now, everyone in the room was listening to our conversation with great interest. As I sat myself on the floor and began to push my hips back against the wall, a crowd gathered around to watch.

"This is one of the best ways to see the difference," I explained. "Now watch closely as I scoot back as far as I can against this wall, extend both my legs as far forward as possible, and there—see?"

All eyes were focused on my upturned feet; the right one extended a good two inches farther than the left.

"Wow," said Heath, "that's neat."

"Yeah," I murmured, suddenly feeling a bit of a freak and very depressed. "Real neat."

Returning to the sofa and sitting down, I sighed.

Madelyn came over and perched on the sofa's arm.

"You know, Cheryl," she said, "this isn't the first time I've seen a short leg like yours. And the ones I've seen were healed."

"Healed?" I asked. "How?"

"Prayer," she answered simply. "In my prayer group there are miracles that happen every week. Not that all are so remarkable as lengthened legs, but I have seen such things happen."

I glanced over at Mother and Daddy to see what their reaction to Madelyn's words might be. Neither were paying attention.

"Well, uh, tell me more," I said. "This sounds pretty interesting."

"Skedaddle over," said Madelyn, as she sat down next to me. "I've got some things I'd like to show you."

With that, she pulled out of her handbag a tiny pocket Bible and began ruffling through its tissue-thin pages.

"Now some folks," she said, "do not believe that God is still in the miracle-working business. But I am among those folks who believe otherwise. As I understand it, Jesus Christ is the same living being He was when He walked the earth two thousand years ago; therefore, He remains more than capable of working the same wonderful miracles as He did back then. Remember all the healings He worked? The man with the withered hand [Matthew 12:9–13, Mark 3:1–5, Luke 6:6–10], the epileptic boy [Matthew 17:14–18, Mark 9:17–27, Luke 9:37–42], the woman with the issue of blood [Matthew 9:20–22, Mark 5:25–34, Luke 8:43–48], and Peter's fevered mother-in-law [Matthew 8:14–17, Mark 1:30–31, Luke 4:38–40]. And these are just a few! Well when Jesus died for us on the cross and rose from the dead, His miracles didn't stop; through the Holy Spirit, He sent His power to the early believers who continued to work miracles—as Jesus had told them earlier that they would—far greater than He had ever done [John 14:12–14]! These are recorded in the Book of Acts."

As Madelyn spoke and read selected passages out loud to me, I felt all tingly with excitement at the implications of what she was saying. I knew already that God was capable of working miracles over long periods of time—that is, things like healing my leg to the point where I was able to walk again and giving Daddy the wisdom to take Heath off his medicine. But to work such graphic miracles such as restoring crippled hands and lengthening short legs—well, it all seemed so dramatic and otherworldly. Still, it was all there, right there in the Bible. And I did believe the Bible.

"It all has to do with faith," Madelyn continued, "in *believing*—not just in your head, but deep down in your spirit—that such things can happen. Jesus understood how hard it was for us as human beings to ever grasp the power of His Father's love. That's why He was forever telling his followers about the importance of faith.

"Look here," she said, "what Jesus said in Mark 11:22–24—Have faith in God. Truly, I say to you, whoever says to this mountain, 'Be taken up and cast into the sea,' and does not doubt in his heart, but believes that what he says will come to pass, it will be done for him. Therefore I tell you, whatever you ask in prayer, believe that you receive it, and you will — RSV.

"Well now, who's to say your short leg isn't just like that mountain? If you believe strongly enough that it will be lengthened, it will. It's all a matter of faith."

"But how does a person get faith?" I asked. "Or get more of it?"

"Faith," answered Madelyn, "comes in one basic way: faith comes from hearing, and hearing by the Word of God. Says so right here in Romans 10:17 (paraphrased). The best way to increase your faith is to read and listen to the Word of God; I like to call it schooling yourself in faith. There's power in the Word — I know you've heard your daddy say that before. Even when you can't feel it happening, the Word — once ingested — begins to work in your spirit. It's kind of like eating an apple; once you've taken a bite, there's a whole mysterious process that begins as your body breaks the apple down into all sorts of chemical and vitamin components that serve to nourish your body. You can't feel it, but it's happening just the same. That's why you've got to school yourself in faith, honey. Your spirit needs feeding if it's going to grow."

"Oh," I said, slightly taken aback by what I was hearing. It all seemed too good to be true—yet it all made perfect sense.

"And one more thing," said Madelyn, her eyes shining with excitement. "This is the best part. Once you've built your faith to the degree where you believe absolutely that God can and will work a miracle, the thing that activates faith is prayer — especially the combined prayers of two or more believers. Jesus explained this principle in Matthew 18:19-20 RSV when he said, 'Again I say to you, if two of you agree on earth about anything they ask, it will be done for them by my Father in heaven. For where two or three are gathered in my name, there am I in the midst of them.'

"Wow," I said, "I never heard any of that before. And you say you've actually seen it work?"

"Indeed I have," Madelyn replied. "There's a prayer meeting over at Mamo's every week that Web and I never miss. [Mamo was Madelyn's and others' nickname for her mother, Lena Cain.] We sing and pray and share what the Lord's been doing in our lives. It's wonderful. We've been meeting on Fridays lately. Why don't you and your family stop by one night?"

"Oh, I don't know," I said doubtfully. It all sounded a little strange to me. "I mean, we're all so busy with rehearsals and concerts, you know. But I am interested in what you've told me about faith and healing. I really am."

"Well then," grinned Madelyn, "start studying that Bible. Start schooling yourself in faith. I guarantee you'll have results. I'll call you every once in a while to see how you're coming along—if you don't mind."

"Oh no," I reassured her, "I don't mind at all. In fact, I'll look forward to it."

"Great," said Madelyn, giving me a squeeze. "Now let's see what the others are up to. I could go for another cup of coffee—and this cinnamon bread is fabulous! Did you have anything to do with it?"

With that, our discussion of spiritual things abruptly ended. In a way, I felt as though I were leaving one world and reentering another as I left the sofa and resumed talking with the others about gospel music, the difficulties of life on the road, and the pros and cons of recording an album.

That night, before going to sleep, I took out a sheet of paper and made a list of all the key scriptural passages that Madelyn had referred to during our discussion about faith and healing. As I looked them up in my Bible, it seemed that such passages were to be found everywhere — even in unexpected places like the Old Testament. In Psalm 103:3 RSV, David wrote of the Lord "who heals all your diseases." And the prophet Isaiah, when describing the nature of the promised Messiah, wrote, "Surely he has borne our griefs and carried our sorrows . . . upon him was the chastisement that made us whole, and with his stripes we are healed'' (Isaiah 53:4-5 RSV). The more I read, the more excited I became; that evening, I stayed up past midnight reading.

A week later Doyle came down from Memphis to introduce us at a county fair. While waiting in the backstage area, a muddy plot littered with discarded Coke cups and Pronto Pup sticks, I mentioned Madelyn's visit—and my growing interest in the possibility of my leg being healed through faith. As I spoke, I was rather surprised by Doyle's obvious enthusiasm. By the time I finished, he was beaming like a thousand-watt bulb.

"Well," I concluded, "what do you think?" Though his glowing expression already answered my question.

"Honey," he said, "I think it's great! I am in perfect agreement with all Madelyn told you. She's a mighty Spirit-filled little lady. Been that way for as long as I can remember, too."

"Then you think it's possible that prayer might heal my leg?" I asked. "You really think so?"

"Sure do," replied Doyle. "No doubt about it."

"Doyle?" I said quietly.

"Yes?" he answered.

"Pray for me," I said. It was the same request I had made to Mother the afternoon of my visit to Dr. Snead. "Pray that I have the faith to believe that Jesus can heal me."

"Of course I will," said Doyle, reaching over and squeezing my hand. "Would be my pleasure. But there's something else you might be thinking about, too."

"What's that?"

"Sometimes we go through difficult times like this for a special reason," he replied. "Often there's an eventual higher good to be gained from the experience—an important lesson to be learned. It could be something even more important than getting healed."

"But what could that be?" I asked. "I don't understand."

"Pray," said Doyle. "Pray for the Lord's wisdom, and He will show you His bigger meaning."

With that, he released my hand.

"Gotta go," he said. "Show time."

"Thanks, Doyle," I called, and I watched him as he scampered up the steps onto the makeshift stage. As I listened to him announce our introduction, I suddenly felt for Doyle a surge of love like I'd never before felt for anyone else in my life. It wasn't romantic love, it wasn't best-friend love, it was something even bigger. The feeling lasted but a second—then was lost in the excitement of running to join Paulette, Tim, and Heath onstage.

For the remainder of the summer, I prayed to God to give me the faith to believe that He could heal me. I read my Bible every day, especially the Gospels—Matthew, Mark, Luke, and John—and the Book of Acts, which contain so many firsthand accounts of miraculous healings. I drilled myself on key passages (especially Mark 11:22–24) and began to listen to tape cassettes of inspirational messages by well-known practitioners of faith healing such as Kenneth Copeland and Kenneth Hagin. Sometimes Mother and Daddy listened, too.

For the most part however, it wasn't an issue I discussed with too many people—with the exception of Madelyn and her prayer-group friends, who frequently called and visited. But it was an issue that was always on my mind. Out of the blue, I'd find myself thinking and praying about it—while working in the garden, baby-sitting with Heath, shopping for patterns and materials with Mother for the upcoming school year.

By early autumn I had reached the point where I did believe—not only in my head, but deep down in my spirit—that the Lord could, and would, heal me. As if to confirm my newfound conviction, one of Madelyn's friends learned that on the evening of October 21 a Christian healing seminar featuring Kenneth Hagin was to be held in Jackson. Highlighting the seminar, which was open to the public, would be preaching by Mr. Hagin and a service where actual healings would take place. Brimming with hope and confidence, I made plans to attend.

In all the excitement, occasionally I'd recall Doyle's suggestion to try and seek a "bigger meaning" that God might want to show me. But not very often. I hadn't seen Doyle in a while; busy with his record and book shop, he was no longer able to travel down to our neck of the woods as often as he had during the summer months. Still, we managed to keep in close touch by telephone; like clockwork, Doyle called me every Saturday from Memphis.

On one such Saturday in late September, the phone rang. Just as I had been hoping, it was Doyle.

"Well, hello there!" he said in his typically cheerful greeting.

We talked and laughed and caught each other up on the latest news. I told Doyle how much I was enjoying my senior year, and how I was looking forward to the Kenneth Hagin seminar. Doyle told me that Lavez had gone to Chicago to visit their daughter, Kay, and how much he was looking forward to a lazy weekend of puttering around on their farm. (There was nothing Doyle loved more than to don old clothes, roll out the tractor, and play farmer.) As usual, the two of us talked a little too long, and hung up in haste. But it was a good call.

That's why I was surprised when later that same day I picked up the phone to hear Doyle's voice again. This time, however, his greeting was uncharacteristically distant.

"Hey, honey," he said, "how're you doing?"

"Doyle!" I exclaimed. "I'm doing fine—nothing's changed since we last talked. What brings you to call again?"

"Well," he replied, "I can't rightly say—" His voice

seemed unusually far away. For a few moments he said nothing. Then, "I thought maybe you'd like to hear a song," he said softly. "Would you like to hear a song?"

"Sure," I replied, slightly disturbed by the underlying sadness to Doyle's voice. And when he began to sing, I almost cried. The song was "The Unseen Hand," a poignantly beautiful tune about trusting God, even to death. Doyle's tremulous voice, as he sang *a cappella*, was tinged with emotion.

"I'm trusting to this unseen hand," he sang, "that guides me through this weary land. And some sweet day I know I'll go, still guided by the unseen hand . . ."

"Doyle," I whispered, when he had finished, "are you all right?" To my dismay, all I heard were sobs on the other end of the line.

"Doyle!" I cried, my own eyes filling with tears. "What's wrong? What's the matter?"

"Don't know, exactly," he replied. "It's hard to explain. But I just want you to know, darlin', how much I love you. You mean an awful lot to me, you know. An awful lot."

"Oh, Doyle," I answered, "I love you, too. I feel the same for you as you do for me. I thank God every day that He brought us together. Our friendship is a precious and beautiful thing."

"Yes it is," said Doyle softly. "That it is, indeed."

Shortly later, we said good-bye. I had returned the receiver about halfway from my ear to the phone, when I heard Doyle say something else.

"What?" I asked, hastily bringing the receiver to my ear. But it was too late. Doyle had hung up. As sweet as our conversation had been, it left me feeling disturbed and vaguely anxious—as though something bad was about to happen. Pushing aside such fears, I went about my work.

On Tuesday evening, after the last of my piano students

had gone, Mother called to me from the kitchen where she and Daddy had been talking since suppertime.

"Your Daddy's got something to tell you," she said. "It's bad news, Cheryl. I think you better sit down."

I sat down.

"We got a call from the Blackwoods today," said Daddy. "It seems that Doyle had an accident last Sunday; while attaching a hitch to his tractor, he fell off and hit his head. When Lavez came home from Chicago that night, she found him lying on the living room floor, just by the front door. She rushed him to the hospital, but in the meantime he suffered some kind of stroke. He's in the hospital now, in a coma."

"What?" I cried, both horrified at the news and furious that Mother and Daddy had known about it for most the day. "Why didn't you tell me earlier? How could you do such a thing?"

"We didn't want you to worry," said Daddy. "We knew you had students to teach."

"Worry?" I cried, bursting into tears. "He's only my best friend in the whole world! We've got to go to Memphis, Daddy. We've got to go see Doyle before it's too late."

"Now hold on just a minute," said Daddy gently, placing a restraining hand on my shoulder. "I understand how you're feeling, but I don't see any need for us to go rushing up to Memphis right this minute. If you'll just agree to lie down and get a few hours sleep, we can leave first thing in the morning. We'll get there in plenty of time that way. All right?"

"I don't know," I said. "I'm so confused. Oh, Daddy, this is all so horrible!"

"There now, baby," said Daddy, leaving his chair and coming around to surround me with his big arms. "Everything's gonna be all right. Don't you worry. Just get yourself some sleep and we'll be in Memphis before you know it."

So I went to bed, but I couldn't sleep. All night long I cried in my pillow, until the pale light of dawn began to fill my room at 6:00 A.M. I was still crying as I packed my overnight bag and headed out to the car with Daddy. I continued crying all the way to Memphis.

When we arrived at the hospital, we headed straight to the intensive care unit where Doyle was staying. A bit further down the corridor from intensive care was the prayer room, where we had been told members of the family were gathered. But just as we reached intensive care, the doors swung open and a doctor appeared. Upon seeing us, he stopped.

"You folks looking for Doyle Blackwood?" he asked.

"Yes, sir," replied Daddy, "we are."

"I'm sorry," said the doctor. "He just died."

I don't exactly remember what happened next—as we followed the doctor into the prayer room, everything seemed to melt into a blur of Blackwoods—Lavez, Kay, Mamo, Madelyn—all falling into each other's arms, their faces contorted with inexpressible grief. Stricken by the sound of their mournful cries and uncontrollable sobs, I stood, riveted by the scene, unable to speak or move. What was there to say? What was there to do? With Doyle dead, it was as though, for me, the world had ended. As though I had died, too.

The funeral took place on Friday, October 4. With that over, I hoped that perhaps the worst was behind us. But for the longest time, the tiniest recollection of Doyle—his smiling eyes in the photograph I kept on my dresser, the sight of a little red truck, the melody of one of our favorite songs on the radio—was enough to unleash a torrent of tears and feelings of anguish, grief, and loss like I'd never known.

Many nights I stayed awake thinking about our final phone conversation. . . . *Could Doyle have somehow known that he was going to die? And what,* I wondered, *were those last words he had spoken to me that I had failed to hear?* Though I knew deep in my soul that Doyle was now at peace with

Jesus, I sometimes doubted that the gaping hole his passing had torn in my heart would ever mend. For a long time, his death remained a subject too painful for me to discuss with anyone—not even Mother or Daddy.

Sometimes my reaction to Doyle's passing surprised me. After all, his wasn't my first experience with death; first, of course, had been Miss Osie Mae, and then, earlier this year, both Daddy's mother and father had died within a month of each other after long illnesses. Sad as these deaths had been, for some reason they had been much easier for me to accept and at least try to understand.

One thing I did know for sure: there would never be another Doyle. And I—like all whose lives he touched—would never be the same for having known him.

IN THE DAYS following Doyle's death, I came to regard the upcoming healing seminar in Jackson as the light at the end of a very long, very dark tunnel. It was, I think, the single most important thing that kept me from completely succumbing to despair.

As the date, Monday, October 21, approached, Madelyn and her friends continued to call and encourage me. In preparation, I kept on reading my Bible and listening to tapes. I kept on praying to God for increased faith.

But the Sunday evening before the seminar found me sitting up in bed, anxious and unable to sleep.

I reached to turn on my bedstand lamp and drew my comforter up tightly under my chin. *What was wrong?* Just a few hours earlier I'd been feeling great—happily chattering with Madelyn in eager anticipation for the coming day. Over time, I'd come to regard the seminar as a big, beautiful, gift-wrapped present just waiting to be opened—the healing within as God's special gift just for me. *Surely*, I thought, *I must be the luckiest girl in the world.*

But I sure didn't feel like the luckiest girl in the world. A vague feeling of disquiet washed over me. Something was definitely not right. And it wasn't a delayed pang of grief for Doyle that I was experiencing; that was a feeling that I had come to know all too well. This was different. Though I couldn't quite put my finger on it, I felt as though something was—missing.

Suddenly Mother poked her head in the doorway.

"You still awake?" she asked. "Don't you think you'd better be getting some sleep? Tomorrow's a big day, you know."

"Yeah," I said dejectedly, "I know."

Mother came over and sat quietly on the edge of my bed.

"Thinking about Doyle?" she asked softly.

"No," I replied, "I don't know what it is that's bothering me. I mean, I believe that tomorrow is going to be a great day and that I will be healed—but I'm just not as excited about it as I thought I would be. Fact is, I feel a little down about the whole thing."

"Hm-m." Mother reached over and stroked the side of my head. "Honey," she said thoughtfully, "didn't you once tell me about a day last summer—I think it was at a fair—when Doyle mentioned something to you about looking for a bigger meaning in this whole healing experience? Something about praying for the Lord's wisdom in the matter?"

"Yes," I answered, "that's true." The interlude was something I hadn't thought about in what seemed like a long time.

"Well, maybe it's something worth thinking about," said Mother. "I can't say I know exactly what he had in mind—but knowing Doyle, you can bet it was something he felt was very important."

"Maybe you're right," I said. "Maybe it is worth considering."

"Well," said Mother, standing up and heading toward the door, "it couldn't hurt. But whatever you do, promise you won't stay up too late, all right?" She stood in the doorway.

"Promise," I replied. "Good night, Mother—and thanks."

Maybe Mother was right, I thought. Again I recalled the "bigger meaning" that Doyle had encouraged me to find and that had so far eluded me. *Maybe this was the source of my unrest.*

Staring blankly at the two little peaks that were my toes beneath the blanket, I tried to shrug my restlessness away. But it persisted, insistent, as if to say, "Come on, Cheryl, you can do it. You can find that deeper meaning."

Finally, as a last resort, I reached for my Bible. I figured I'd read until I fell asleep. Maybe I'd even gain a little insight. Opening the book, I turned to John, my favorite Gospel. When I came to the fourteenth chapter, twenty-ninth verse, my heart did a little flip-flop. Jesus was speaking to His disciples, but He might as well have been addressing me face to face.

"And now," He said, "I have told you before it takes place, so that when it does take place, you may believe."

Jesus was telling His disciples of future events that were to take place—specific, unusual occurrences—in order that when they happened, the disciples would believe in Him.

Amazing! I thought. *Could this be what the Lord wanted me to do with the healing I expected? Could it be that He wanted me to somehow use it as a witness to His reality in today's world?*

At first the idea made me apprehensive. What would some of my friends think? Religion for so many folks was such a touchy subject. Besides, more than a few boys were still calling me "preacher girl." But as I read and reread the verse, I brushed my fears aside. By the time I fell asleep, it was clear in my mind what I had to do.

As I placed my books in my school locker the next morning, my heart was beating a little faster than usual. Looking down the corridor, I caught a glimpse of my good friend Dolly Chambers. I guess I'd known Dolly, a cheerleader, for about three years. Once she'd asked if she could go to church with me. For one reason or another, we never got around to doing it. Now it occurred to me that she'd never again raised the question.

"Dolly!" I called, motioning her toward me with my arm. "Got a minute?"

"Hey, Cheryl," she responded, "what's up?"

"C'mere," I said. "I want to show you something."

Dolly's eyebrows shot skyward as she watched me plunk myself down on the linoleum hallway, push my back up against the wall of lockers, and extend my legs straight forward.

"What are you doing?" she laughed.

"Now Dolly," I said, "I want to show you something. You may have noticed I have a slight limp, right?"

"Well—uh, yes," she replied, "but it doesn't amount to much."

"Well," I interrupted, "it's because of my leg. My left leg. It's short. I was in an accident when I was little, and it made my leg short."

"Oh, you poor thing," cried Dolly, "I never knew—"

"No, no, Dolly!" I protested. "Don't feel sorry. The reason I'm showing you this is because tomorrow morning these legs are going to be the same length."

"What?" Dolly looked confused.

"My leg is going to be healed," I said. "I've been praying about it all summer, and I believe God can heal me. That's the reason I'm telling you this—so that when it happens, you'll know Who's responsible."

"Whatever you say, Cheryl." Dolly grinned wryly. "I'll believe it when I see it."

"And you will," I said earnestly. "You really will!"

"You're too much," laughed Dolly, as she turned to head for class. "Catch you later."

By lunchtime, I guess I'd had similar conversations with about ten other kids, and, by the end of the day, five or six more. Reactions varied from, "C'mon, Cheryl, you've got to be kidding" to "Really? I didn't know that kind of miracle stuff was still going on—tell me more!"

That evening, Madelyn Wood and four other friends picked me up at four-thirty, for the two-hour drive to Jackson. Mother and Daddy stayed home.

As we headed south on the Natchez Trace Parkway, Madelyn suggested that we get the evening off to a good start with a prayer. One of the men passengers, Mr. Wayne Melton, obliged, both thanking the Lord for the opportunity to attend the seminar and asking Him to protect us in our journey. Then, also at Madelyn's suggestion, one by one each passenger began to share first-hand stories of healing experiences; Web Wood had been cured of emotional problems, Mamo of a badly sprained ankle, and Mr. Melton of debilitating allergies. We sang some songs, and before we knew it we were approaching Jackson's city limits. Just before arriving at our destination, Madelyn—who had been to healing seminars before—gave me a little idea of what to expect.

"There'll be some singing," she said. "And lots of praying. And don't be surprised if you hear some folks speaking or singing in a language that doesn't sound like English."

I had no idea what Madelyn meant by her last comment, but the closer we got to the seminar, the more I thought I felt a warm, tingling sensation all over my left leg. This, however, I mentioned to no one—attributing it to an overactive imagination.

The seminar, attended by some five hundred people, was held in a large meeting room in Jackson's old Heidelberg Hotel. A wide aisle separated the sea of folding chairs into two major areas, and we found our seats in the front right section. I guess I was pretty excited at the session's start, when Kenneth Hagin walked on to the speaking platform and began to preach on faith. And at one point, when he asked any members of the audience who wanted to receive the Holy Spirit to form a line and meet with assistants in another room, I jumped to my feet.

"Hold it!" cried Madelyn, reaching up to pull me back. "That's not for you. You came for the healing service."

"Oh," I laughed. "Sorry."

By the time the healing service began, I'd more or less calmed down.

People desiring healings were asked by Mr. Hagin to come down to the front of the room and form a line in front of the speaking platform. With a good-bye wave, I left my seat and found a place somewhere in the middle. Then Mr. Hagin began working his way down the line, laying his hands on and praying over each person individually.

The healings were quiet, low key, and not overly emotional. Sometimes friends and family members stood close by the person being healed. Some of the healings had to do with internal or emotional illnesses; in these cases, the only outward indications that anything had happened were the transformed expressions of the people when they returned to their seats. Their faces radiated a quality of peace and joy I'd never seen. Often their eyes sparkled with tears of happiness. The more I watched, the more eager I became for my turn.

"Now don't you think about me," I heard Mr. Hagin saying as he prayed over people. "I want you to focus all your thoughts toward Jesus."

I did.

"Thank You, Jesus," I prayed. "Thank You for loving me. Thank You for bringing me here this evening. Thank You for wanting to heal me. Praise You, Lord Jesus . . ."

As I continued praising and thanking Jesus, I suddenly became aware that I was no longer speaking in English, but in another, more beautiful, more graceful language that seemed to flow from the depths of my spirit in swirls and eddies of indescribable joy. To speak in this new and unknown tongue was effortless; moreover, for all its inherent grace and beauty, it seemed all the more effective and appropriate as a means of expressing the praise I felt. *Could this,* I wondered, *be the language of angels?*

Suddenly, Mr. Hagin was standing before me.

"Now don't you think about me," he was saying softly. "I want you to focus all your thoughts on Jesus."

Gently, firmly, he placed his hands on my head. A great sense of security, peace—confidence in what was about to take place—surged through me.

"In the name of Jesus," he prayed . . .

I never heard him finish.

Soothing warmth, as though I'd been immersed in a hot tub, enveloped me. For a moment I seemed to lose track of time. I was aware in my mind that Mr. Hagin was still by my side, but somehow I no longer heard a word he was saying. It was as though I had slipped away to some faraway bright-shining place—a private place inhabited only by myself and Jesus. I felt overwhelmed, filled to overflowing, with His Presence—with His power, compassion, and love. More than anything else, His love.

Closing my eyes, I felt myself sink to the floor. Someone must have been standing behind me to catch me and gently lay me down. Stretched out on the floor, as though in a deep sleep, my legs were extended straight forward.

What happened next, I'll never forget.

In wonder, I sat up and opened my eyes to see that my left leg had extended until my heels, like two perfectly matched bookends, were now suddenly side by side. In a matter of seconds, after six long years, my legs were of equal length! I had been healed!

"Thank You, Jesus," I whispered. "Oh, thank You!"

Leaping up, I stamped my left foot on the floor to make sure that what I'd seen was really true. Over and over I stamped my foot, each resounding thump a triumphant affirmation of my healing.

"He did it!" I cried. "He did it!" Tears of joy streamed down my face as I ran back to join the others. "Jesus did it! He healed my leg!"

"Well, praise the Lord!" cried Madelyn, as she and the others gathered around me. "Show us! Show us!"

Laughing, I stamped my foot and skipped down the aisle.

"Never could do that before," I said breathlessly. "Never. C'mon," I grabbed Madelyn's hands and pulled her toward the meeting-room door. "Let's go out in the hallway, where I can show you better."

Undaunted by gawking onlookers (those folks who were in the Heidelberg Hotel for reasons other than the Kenneth Hagin seminar) I sat down on the floor next to the nearest wall, pushed my back up against it as far as I could and extended my legs forward. Again, my heart leapt with happiness as I saw how my feet, from heels to toe, were perfectly even.

"Look at that!" I cried to people passing by, as I pointed to my legs. "Perfectly even! I've been healed, you see. I've been healed of a short leg!"

I didn't even care about the people who looked at me as though I was crazy and who then—upon seeing my adult friends and assuming they were my legal guardians—shook their heads sadly and walked away. I didn't care about the woman who thought I was drunk. All I cared about was the fact that I had been healed. I had experienced a personal encounter with Jesus more love-filled and powerful than I had ever dreamed was possible, and *I had been healed!*

"Cheryl, honey," said Madelyn, reaching down to help me up, "before this evening is over, Mr. Hagin will be getting together another group of people who want to receive the Holy Spirit. Would you like me to tell you what that's all about and then perhaps consider it?"

"Oh," I said, suddenly recalling the beautiful unknown language that I had spoken when praising and thanking Jesus prior to my healing. "I think—I think I've already got it."

"You do?" asked Madelyn. "Tell us about it!"

At first I felt shy talking about my experience; it seemed so unusual and intimate. But as soon as I began to tell Madelyn and the others what had happened, all fears dissolved in light of their enthusiastic response.

"Land sakes!" cried Madelyn, when I had finished my story. "You sure did receive the Holy Spirit!" She laughed. "You, my dear, are one blessed child! Let's hurry on home so you can tell everyone the good news!"

While in the car, I got to thinking about Doyle. My eyes filled with tears. *If only Doyle could have been with us this evening*, I thought. *How happy he would have been!*

"Madelyn," I said, my voice choking with emotion, "I sure wish Doyle could have been with us tonight. I wish there was some way to let him know what's happened."

"Cheryl," she responded softly, "it's my belief that Doyle does know. For a long time now, I've believed that God lets all His children in Heaven know whenever good things happen to their loved ones here on earth. That's an important part of their paradise."

It must have been one o'clock in the morning by the time we arrived home, but all of us were still high as kites with excitement as we pulled into the driveway. Madelyn had barely stopped the car when I pushed open my door.

"Bye!" I called, as I raced to the house. "Talk to you tomorrow!"

Flying into Mother's bedroom I was surprised to find her sitting up in bed, reading.

"Look, Mother," I cried, dancing around the bed. "He did it! Jesus healed my leg! He really did it!"

"What?" said Mother, adjusting her glasses. "Jesus did what? Now Cheryl, honey, calm yourself. It's mighty late you know. I wish you'd told me you were going to be so late. I haven't been able to sleep for worrying when you were going to get back."

"Mother," I cried, "listen to me! Look! I've been healed!"

"My Lord," said Mother, in a hushed tone, as she realized for the first time what had, indeed, taken place. "I knew you were certain that you'd get your healing, but I—I wasn't really so sure—"

"Where's Daddy?" I cried. "We've got to show Daddy!"

By now, Tim and Heath, wakened by the noise, were standing outside the bedroom door, peering into the room. Behind them I could see Daddy's silver head.

"Daddy!" I cried.

"What in tarnation," he bellowed, "is going on here?"

"I'm healed!" I said, pushing my way past Tim and Heath and throwing my arms around Daddy. "Jesus healed my leg, Daddy. He really did."

"Hosea," said Mother, who had gotten out of bed and was pulling on her robe, "it's true. I do believe what Cheryl says is true."

"I've got to call Paulette," I said, releasing my hold around Daddy and running down the hall. Paulette, who had in the past year suffered a short-lived marriage and a divorce, was now a student of pharmaceutics at Ole Miss. "She's gonna be so excited!"

As I dialed her number, the others filed past and into the living room.

"Paulette?" I said, as I heard her say hello. "It's me, Cheryl. I've been healed, Paulette! I went to a healing seminar with Madelyn and the man prayed over me, and my leg grew!"

"That's real nice, Cheryl," mumbled Paulette, groggy with sleep. "I'll believe it when I see it."

"Oh," I said, my spirits not dampened in the least by her skeptical response, "you will, Paulette. You really will!"

That night, the rest of us stayed up for about an hour as I told and retold the events of the evening. After running, skipping, and pushing myself up against the wall to prove my point, I finally ran upstairs and pulled on a pair of slacks as final evidence. Sure enough, falling well above my ankle, my left-leg hemline was now a good two inches too high.

"Well!" exclaimed Mother, upon seeing the difference. "Looks like I've got a lot of sewing to do!"

When I returned to school the next morning wearing a newly hemmed pair of slacks and walking with a decidedly improved gait, reactions from students and teachers were varied. Some believed. Some didn't. Some wanted to know more.

When I met up with my friend Dolly and showed her what had happened, she got real quiet. She looked at my legs for what must have been a full minute before raising her eyes to speak.

"You know, Cheryl," she said, "about your leg—"

"Yes?" I said.

"Remember yesterday when I told you, 'I'll believe it when I see it'?"

"Yes," I said, "I remember."

"Well," she said quietly, "now I've seen." She paused. "And I believe."

"Oh, Dolly!" I cried, hugging her tightly. "You don't know what that means to me!"

Tears filled our eyes, and I was filled with gratitude—not only for Dolly's new faith, but for my newfound understanding of the "bigger meaning" behind my experience: more meaningful than my healing was the fact that there is a God—a living, powerful, personal God—Who delights in doing such things! The ultimate reason for answered prayers of any kind (especially miracles) is to serve as a sign to others (especially nonbelievers) of God's existence and love.

As if that weren't enough, later physical examinations by both Dr. Snead and a general practitioner revealed that my ability to bear children was the same as any ordinary woman's. Whether or not it had at one time been impaired, it was Dr. Snead's warning that had served as the impetus for me to ultimately seek a total healing from God—and for that I remain forever thankful.

Without a doubt, my healing experience was the most extraordinary event of my life. But in ensuing days, I began to sense that it was merely a drop in the ocean of Christian experience—an ocean in whose spiritual waters I'd barely begun to submerge my big toe. It seemed I had so many questions—

especially about this strange and wonderful person called the Holy Spirit. I wanted to know more.

"Madelyn," I said, a week or so following my healing, "about this person called the Holy Spirit—there's so much I don't understand. I mean, I know when I was healed that I had the experience of speaking in another language, 'speaking in tongues,' I've heard you call it. And I know that since then I've continued to pray that way in private—not only is it satisfying in itself, but it also seems to have the additional effect of building up my faith. But where does it come from? Does it serve any other purposes? Is it mentioned in the Bible? There's so much more I want to know."

Curled up on the sofa in the music room, we were in much the same position as when Madelyn, months earlier, had first explained to me about God's ability and desire to heal. Now, I almost had to laugh as I saw her reach for her little pocket Bible and once again begin to riffle through its well-worn pages. I could feel the excited stirring of her spirit as she began to speak.

"Now some folks," she said, fixing her green eyes on mine, "do not believe the Holy Spirit and all His related spiritual gifts are active and available for use by today's believers. However, I am among those folks who believe otherwise.

"Before Jesus died," she continued, "He promised His disciples that He would not leave them desolate, but at an appointed time following His death and resurrection, He would send to them His Holy Spirit to serve as their counselor and guide unto all truth [John 14:15–25]. This arrival of the Holy Spirit was so important to Jesus that He again reminded His disciples about it during the forty-day period when he appeared on earth in His resurrected form [Acts 1:3–5]. The big event finally took place when the disciples were gathered in the holy city of Jerusalem to observe the Jewish day of Pentecost, when, as recorded in Acts 2:2–4, 'suddenly a sound came from heaven like the rush of a mighty wind, and it filled all the house where they were sitting. And there appeared to them tongues as of fire, distributed and resting on each one of them. And they were all filled with the Holy Spirit and began to speak in other tongues, as the Spirit gave them utterance. RSV' "

"Really?" I asked. "But why? Why did God give them the gift of other languages?"

"In this case," replied Madelyn, "it was because there were also many nonbelievers of Christ—Jews from many nations—who had gathered for Pentecost in Jerusalem, and when they heard the great noise of the Holy Spirit's arrival, they all came running. To their amazement, they found that the disciples, all Galileans, were praising God and exalting Christ in the various languages of their native lands [Acts 2:5-13]. While some mocked the disciples, thinking they were drunk with new wine, others were convinced—and about three thousand were added to the ranks of believers that day, and all because of the Holy Spirit [Acts 2:37-42]."

"Wow!" I said. "That's really something. But Madelyn, the tongues spoken by the disciples at Pentecost were for the ears of those people in the crowd who could translate. When I speak my language in prayer, I have no idea what I'm saying. I only know that it just comes naturally—I can start it and stop it at will—and it's especially helpful when I feel like praising the Lord or praying for reasons so deep that I have a hard time articulating what I want to say in words."

"I think your private use of tongues reflects what Paul meant when he wrote, 'He who speaks in a tongue edifies himself' [I Corinthians 14:4 RSV].'' said Madelyn. ''There's a certain element of completely yielding yourself to God in the very act that's both humbling and awesome. The language, which you know you aren't making up, is a very real reminder of God's power and presence. But there is another use of tongues, too, you know. In a body of believers an individual may be inspired to speak in tongues in order than another member of the body who has the gift of interpretation may translate—for the edification of everyone [1 Corinthians 14:27]."

"Wait a minute," I said, "the gift of *interpretation?* You mean there are other gifts of the Holy Spirit?"

"Oh, yes!" cried Madelyn. "There are so many—the list is practically endless. Some seem more spectacular for their supernatural quality—gifts such as tongues, interpretation, healing, prophecy, and the working of miracles. But equally inspired and important are the Holy Spirit's gifts of wisdom, teaching, hospitality, and so on. All are gifts from the same God. All are inspired by the same Holy Spirit. And all are appropriated differently in each believer, for the overall good of the body in general [1 Corinthians 12]. But it's always important to remember that all the gifts—no matter how spectacular—pale in the light of love. All are worth absolutely nothing if the believer's motivation for seeking and using them is anything less than love [1 Corinthians 13]."

Madelyn paused, as if to catch her breath.

"The exciting thing about speaking in tongues," she said, while taking hold of both my hands, "is that it often proves to be a doorway into a deeper experience of the other gifts. In a sense, that's what happened with you at the Kenneth Hagin seminar; in praise, you surrendered yourself to tongues and, in doing so, opened yourself up enough to let God heal you. It's so exciting, Cheryl. Who knows what more He might have in store for you?"

"But Madelyn," I said, my head spinning with all the information I had received, "before I got filled with the Holy Spirit, before I spoke in tongues, before I was ever healed—wasn't I a Christian then, too?"

"What do you think?" asked Madelyn, softly.

For a moment, I was silent—recalling the events that had led to my encounter with the Holy Spirit. When suddenly, I was overwhelmed with the realization that it was none other than *Jesus* Who had led me to the experience. Step by step, He had led me—working through the situations and people He had chosen to bring into my life at His appointed time.

"Of course I was a Christian!" I exclaimed. "What a silly question! It's just that now my faith seems somehow more real—and a lot more exciting."

"You're so right," said Madelyn. "That's what people mean when they speak of the 'fullness' of the Holy Spirit. That's what Jesus meant, I think, when He said, 'I came that they may have life, and have it abundantly' [John 10:10 RSV]."

"But what about people who never go to a Kenneth Hagin seminar or have a friend like you?" I asked. "How do they ever find out about the Holy Spirit?"

"Well," said Madelyn thoughtfully, "I really do believe that it's God's desire that all His children experience the Christian life to its fullest; there are lots of books about the Holy Spirit, and more and more it seems that individuals everywhere are having experiences not unlike yours. Some people call this trend the 'Charismatic Movement' (the word 'charismatic' coming from the Greek word *charismata*, meaning 'gifts'), but I've never been one too fond of labels. The way I see it, once God has put the desire in someone's heart to get to know His Holy Spirit, that person inevitably will.

"Basically," she concluded, "all a person has to do is ask—ask the Lord for a deeper relationship with His Holy Spirit.

"It's as simple as that," she smiled, closing her Bible and returning it to her pocketbook. "As simple as a prayer."

A FEW WEEKS after my healing, I went downstairs to breakfast to find Daddy's chair empty, his place at the table not set. This was unusual; when it came to meals, Daddy was typically not only the first to arrive, but also the last to leave.

"Mother," I said, dropping my school books on the floor next to my chair, "where's Daddy? There's nothing wrong with him, is there?"

"Sh-h-h," said Mother, putting her finger to her lips. "Your daddy woke up with one of his sick headaches. He's upstairs trying to get some rest."

"That's too bad," I said. "Did you-all try praying?"

"Hm?" asked Mother. In the midst of mashing yams for supper's sweet potato pie, she was only half listening.

"Did you try praying?" I repeated. "God doesn't want Daddy hurting, you know. Prayers can make him well."

"No, dear," said Mother, a hint of exasperation in her voice, "we didn't try praying."

"You didn't?" I cried. "Well, why not? I'm going upstairs right now and seeing to it that Daddy gets prayed for."

"Cheryl," said Mother, "I don't think that's a very good idea—"

But already I was out of hearing range, dashing up the stairs and into Daddy's darkened room. Though both Mother and Daddy believed that I had truly been healed by God, neither of them fully shared my enthusiasm for prayer and the Holy Spirit. I couldn't understand why.

"Daddy?" I said, approaching the side of his bed.

"Hey, honey." He extended his hand. "How're you doing this morning?"

"I'm doing fine," I said, "but Mother told me you've got another one of your sick headaches."

Not bothering to open his eyes, Daddy nodded.

"Well," I said, in my most businesslike voice, "there's no

need for you to be sick, you know. All you've got to do is build up your faith and pray. Pray to God, and He'll make you better!"

"That's nice," murmured Daddy. "That's real nice, Cheryl —but I'm not feeling too good right now. I, uh, think you'd better leave."

"But Daddy—"

I was silenced, however, as he opened his eyes and shot me one of his sterner expressions.

"Okay," I said, releasing my hand from his and moving away from the bed. "But I don't understand why you and Mother don't even *try* to pray. You-all don't know what you're missing!"

As I left the room and entered the hallway, I bumped into Tim, who was scowling and holding his right hand to his cheek.

"What's the matter with you?" I asked. "You don't look so good."

"Toothache," he replied glumly. "I just told Mother about it and she called the dentist. The appointment's in half an hour. Boy, if there's anything I hate, it's going to the dentist."

"But, Tim," I said, "Why'd you bother to tell Mother? We could have just prayed for your toothache, and it would have gotten better."

"Aw, c'mon, Cheryl," said Tim, "when are you going to cut it out? All this talk about praying and healing and the Holy Spirit—if you want to know the truth, we're getting pretty sick of it. It's all you've talked about for the past three weeks, and it's getting boring."

"You just hush, Tim Prewitt," I said. "You don't even know what you're talking about. None of you do. You just don't understand, that's all."

Refusing to carry the conversation further, Tim, shaking

his head in disgust, walked down the hall to his bedroom and closed the door.

Frustrated, I went downstairs and ate my breakfast alone in silence. Not bothering to say good-bye to Mother, I picked up my books and walked to the bus stop. While waiting for the bus, I thought about Tim and his remarks, but doing so just made me angry, so I pushed them out of my mind.

Early that morning, on the way to my locker, I ran into my friend Angela. Usually vivacious, she looked a little under the weather.

"Anything the matter?" I asked.

"Oh, nothing much," she responded. "Just a little stomachache. Hope I'm not catching anything."

"Say," I said, "we've both got study hall this morning. Why don't we meet there a little early and take a few moments to pray? You'll be feeling better in no time!"

"Gosh, Cheryl," said Angela, her expression both curious and concerned, "I don't think so. I mean, I—uh, I've got to stay late and talk with one of my teachers before study hall. I'll be too late. But thanks anyway, Cheryl. Really, thanks for thinking of me."

Later that afternoon, as I finished my piano lesson with Becky, I was about to get up from the bench to go home when I felt her hand on my arm.

"Cheryl," she said softly, "I'd like you to stay for a few minutes. There's something I want to discuss with you."

"Sure," I said, swinging myself around on the piano bench to face her. "What is it?"

"Well," she said, "I don't know exactly how to tell you this, but—I mean, we've been friends for a long time, right?"

"Right," I agreed.

"Well, sometimes," said Becky, "a friend just has to be honest, even though being honest might hurt the other person. And the last thing I'd ever want to do is hurt you, Cheryl, but—"

"Becky," I interrupted, wondering what in the world could cause her such difficulty in speaking to me. "What is it? Please tell me. Tell me flat out."

"Well," said Becky, drawing in her breath, "it's about your healing, and all this talk about the Holy Spirit."

"Oh," I said, trying to ignore the sinking sensation in the pit of my stomach.

"Cheryl," Becky went on, "people are beginning to talk about you—not only kids, but teachers, too. They think it's great that your short leg got lengthened, but all this talk about prayer, and healing, and the Holy Spirit—not only do they think it's weird, but you're putting them off with it! Now I know you, Cheryl; I know how much it means to you to be liked by people, and I know what a great girl you *are*. But honey, if you keep this up—well, you're going to be the one that winds up hurt and lonely, and I'd hate to see that happen."

For a moment I was stunned by Becky's words—not so much by what she had said, but by the fact that she had spoken to me at all about the matter. Though we were exceedingly close, our friendship was based on our mutual interest in music and school-related activities; only in the broadest terms did we ever discuss religion.

Still, as I weighed Becky's comments, I realized that she was right. I had been pushy with my faith—not only at home, but at school, too. Like a steamroller, I had tried to force my beliefs on everyone, from Tim to my teachers, never stopping to think that not everyone shared my enthusiasm and—worse—that I might be pushing them even farther away from the truths I knew by my aggressive behavior.

"Cheryl," said Becky, "are you all right?"

"Yeah," I said gloomily. "Just call me your local fanatic."

"Come on, now," said Becky, smiling, "it's not that bad.

At least not now that we're doing something about it. I realize it's not often you and I discuss religion, but there's a little story I'd like to share with you—one I think that will shed some light on this whole problem."

I watched as Becky pulled an old black Bible out from beneath her stacks of songbooks. It must have been there all along, but I'd never noticed it before.

"I had a friend once," said Becky, "a Christian girl like yourself, who was dating a boy who wasn't a believer. Well, that girl did everything under the sun to try and get her boyfriend to see the truth; she bought him a Bible, she dragged him to church, she insisted upon saying grace at every meal they shared — even a hamburger at McDonald's. For weeks this went on — to no avail; if anything, my friend's zealousness served to turn the boy farther away from God. As you can imagine, this hurt her terribly. At that time, this boy was the most important thing in the world to her. Well, one night she was reading in her Bible in the First Book of Peter about how when Jesus submitted Himself to suffering, He didn't feel a need to threaten his oppressors, but trusted everything to God [I Peter 2:23]. 'Likewise you wives,' the passage continued, 'be submissive to your husbands, so that some, though they do not obey the word, may be won without a word by the behavior of their wives' [I Peter 3:1 RSV]. In other words, actions speak louder than words.

"Well, my friend was so excited about this idea that she could hardly wait to begin to *not* talk about Christianity with her boyfriend. That very night she vowed to simply try to live her life the best she knew how, trusting that this in itself would serve as an effective witness. And do you know what?" Becky closed her Bible and returned it to the stack of books. "That boy accepted Christ into his life one month later."

"I think I get your message," I grinned. "And thanks, Becky, for being such a good friend. You know—I feel just about as excited as your friend did upon hearing that scripture. For the first time in my life, I can't wait to *not* talk, too!

"Now remember I said that," I said, as I stood to leave. "That's one statement I doubt you'll ever hear coming from my mouth again!"

Laughing, Becky walked me to the door. As we said goodbye, we hugged each other tightly.

In the days that followed, I adhered to my vow of silence; that is, instead of trying to do the job myself, I trusted that God—in His own way and in His own time—was working in the hearts of my friends and family to bring them to a closer knowledge of Him and His Holy Spirit. Privately, however, I continued to pray a lot—especially for my family.

Happily, it wasn't too long before the five of us—Mother, Daddy, Tim, Heath, and myself—were regulars at Mamo's Friday night prayer meetings. (These were the meetings that Madelyn had mentioned months earlier.) A typical meeting started after supper, around 7:00 P.M., and was attended by anywhere from fifteen to fifty people. While most meetings usually lasted three hours, some occasionally went on until one or two in the morning, or—as Madelyn put it—"as long as the Spirit moved." Most meetings started with singing and praise. Sometimes we listened to inspirational tapes, but usually we simply took turns sharing how the Lord had been working in our lives during the past week and mentioned prayer requests—both for ourselves and other people. If someone was in particular need of prayer—say, the person had a job problem or needed a healing of some sort—we prayed for him on the spot. When this happened, the person sat in a chair in the middle of the room (I liked to call it the "hot seat") and those who felt so inspired laid their hands on him and prayed. Basically, the meetings were conducted in the spirit of James, when he wrote to New Testament believers, "Is any one among you suffering? Let him pray. Is any cheerful? Let him sing praise. Is any among you sick? Let him call for the elders of the church, and let them pray over him . . ." (James 5:13-14 RSV).

In addition, a wide variety of spiritual gifts were represented among those within the group, and in the course of an evening it wasn't unusual for someone to stand up and prophesy, or "have a word from the Lord." Prophetic utterance, I learned, occurs in a person in much the same way as someone who speaks in tongues, in that the words flow inspired and unrehearsed. In prophecy, however, the language is one understood by the listeners. The message may be for either a specific individual or for the group at large. It was also not uncommon for the prayer meeting to be a place where many received the "baptism of the Holy Spirit" for the first time. (This, I learned, was the common term for a person's initial encounter with speaking in tongues.)

As remarkable and dramatic as such goings on might have seemed, all transpired in matter-of-fact order in the decidedly ordinary atmosphere of Mamo's well-lit living room. Though Mother, Daddy, and the boys had not personally experienced the Holy Spirit in their lives, they, like many others, felt both comfortable and uplifted by the meetings.

The only member of our family who didn't regularly attend the meetings was Paulette. It wasn't that Paulette didn't believe or agree with the specifics of my deepened Christian experience; it was just that Paulette was incapable of getting excited about anything. Upon seeing my lengthened leg, her reaction had been little more than a raised eyebrow. Though more than six years had passed since the accident, depression remained Paulette's continual state of mind; occasional outbursts of anger the only signs of life within.

In January 1975 Paulette came home from Ole Miss a little early one afternoon to rehearse with our singing group. The following day we were booked to perform at a church over in the next county, and featured in the program was a solo by Paulette which still needed a lot of work. The song was "Greater Is He That Is in Me," a tune based on the passage in the First Book of John, which reads, "for he who is in you is greater than he who is in the world" (I John 4:4 RSV). In other words, God's Holy Spirit in a believer is greater than any of Satan's evil in the world. It was an easy enough number, but for some reason, Paulette just couldn't seem to do a decent job of it. Though she had the lyrics down pat, it was the song's spirit of joy and victory that eluded her. Tonight's rehearsal was her last chance to try and get it right; otherwise, we'd simply have to substitute another number.

After an early supper, we gathered in the music room. Wanting to save plenty of time for "Greater Is He That Is in Me," we ran through the rest of the program quickly. Then Paulette sang. Three times she sang. But no matter how hard she tried, it was clear—with her lackluster inflection and unhappy expression—that the number was beyond hope.

"I know, I know," said Paulette, as she put down her microphone. "I know it's a bad job, but I just don't like this song."

"You don't?" asked Heath. "I think it's neat!"

"I don't care what you think," snapped Paulette. "I think it's dumb. To begin with, what does it mean? I mean, what does it mean to say, 'greater is He that is in me'? I don't know what's so great about anything in *me*. It's the same old rotten stuff that's been there for the past seven years. It's the same old junk, day in, day out. I think the song's stupid."

Muttering, she left the room.

"It's all right, baby," I said to Heath, who was still smarting from Paulette's sharp retort. "Paulette doesn't mean anything when she talks like that. She's just got a lot of hurts deep inside her that need mending, that's all. We've got to pray for her." I wrapped my arm around him. "You understand?"

"Yes," he said, "I think so. It's like Paulette got hurt worse than any of us in the car wreck, but she never got better."

"That's right," I said. "That's exactly what it's like."

Our moment together was interrupted by Daddy's booming voice.

"Prayer-meeting time!" he called. "Car leaves in five minutes!"

When I arrived at the car, I was surprised to see Paulette sitting in the back seat next to Tim. It had been a long time since she had last joined us for a meeting. She seemed unusually quiet—but it was a silence more contemplative than moody. Not wanting to disturb her, I said nothing.

About thirty people were at the meeting that night, including Madelyn, Web, and several of those who had gone with me to the Kenneth Hagin seminar. For the most part, the meeting proceeded as usual; first we sang, then we read some scripture, until finally we started sharing and bringing up prayer requests.

That's why I was rather surprised when one of the women in the room suddenly stood up and said, "Excuse me, but I believe there is someone here who desires to receive the Holy Spirit."

For a moment the room was silent.

Then, in a tiny voice, Paulette spoke up.

"Me," she said quietly. "That person is me."

"Well, praise the Lord!" piped Madelyn. "You just get yourself on over to the prayer chair, Paulette, and we'll start praying for you this minute."

Paulette walked over to the chair and sat down. Madelyn, Mamo, and a few others gathered round her. I remained in my seat. Then I watched as folks around the room, including Mother and Daddy, lowered their heads in prayer. I closed my eyes, too.

"In the name of Jesus," I heard someone say, "we ask You,

Father, to fill this child of Yours with Your Holy Spirit, and, in doing so, we also ask that you cast out any evil within her that may be keeping her from knowing Your perfect love. Heal and cleanse her, Father, inside and out—from the top of her head to the tips of her toes. In the name of Your precious Son, Jesus, we pray—Amen!"

In the moments that followed, some of the people in the room began murmuring words of praise and thanksgiving, others began praying softly in tongues. Opening my eyes to join in, I was amazed to see that among those people praying was Paulette—her face radiant with happiness. Tears of joy streamed down her cheeks to meet an ever-widening smile that seemed to shine like the sun, until suddenly the smile broke wide open, and Paulette was laughing! For the first time in seven years, she was actually laughing! For what must have been a full ten minutes, Paulette continued to laugh and cry—first one and then the other—in doing so, releasing all the grief and guilt and unhappiness that had been locked up inside her for so many years.

"Thank You, Jesus," I heard her say. "Oh, thank You, Jesus."

Looking over at Mother and Daddy, I saw that they, too, were smiling at the scene—though Mother's eyes seemed unusually bright and Daddy was reaching for his handkerchief.

Hours later, while riding home in the car, Heath turned around from where he was sitting between Mother and Daddy in the front seat and asked Paulette to describe what had happened.

"Tell us everything, Paulette," he said. "It all seemed so neat!"

"Gosh, Heath," replied Paulette, "it's kind of hard to explain. Though I never mentioned it to any of you, for a long, long time I'd been praying for some way to get the emotional healing I knew I needed and for a closer relationship with

God. After hearing about Cheryl's experience, I wondered if the Holy Spirit might be what I needed, too. That's why I decided to go with you to the prayer meeting.

"Tonight, when that woman spoke up, I knew in my heart it was me she was talking about. And when they prayed over me, it was just as though something inside me popped, and all the junk that had been festering inside me flowed out, and clean sunlight came shining in. Never have I felt so loved by God—still, I've got a feeling this is just the beginning. I know there's so much more in me that remains to be cleaned up and thrown out; but now, with the help of God's Holy Spirit, I feel so much more hopeful!" Paulette paused. "I don't know if that makes any sense to you, Heath, but it's exactly what happened. Basically, I guess I could say I feel like a new person." She grinned. "Bet you're glad to hear that, aren't you?"

"Well—" giggled Heath, "you're the one who said it."

The next afternoon, as we gathered in the music room for a quick conference before leaving for our concert, I asked Paulette how she felt about singing some other song instead of "Greater Is He That Is in Me" as part of the program.

"Cheryl," she said, "you're not going to believe this, but I want to try 'Greater Is He.' I really think I can do it!"

"But Paulette," I protested, "you haven't even had time to rehearse it since yesterday. I don't think it's a very good idea."

"Please," said Paulette. "It's important to me."

"Well," I said, trying not to let my skepticism show, "all right."

Incredibly, Paulette's rendition that day of "Greater Is He That Is in Me" was not only flawless, but also inspired. Never had I heard her sing with more enthusiasm and understanding; she seemed to positively glow with the song's spirit of victory and triumph. Clearly Paulette was a living example of the song's message: the spirit of God's love within her was more than enough to overcome any evil or obstacle in the world.

At the concert's end, nearly half a dozen people became Christians or reaffirmed their commitment to the Lord at the altar rail. I was convinced this happened because of the genuine conviction and love they sensed in Paulette's solo.

In later weeks, one by one, each of the members of my family followed Paulette's lead in receiving the Holy Spirit. (Daddy, as it turned out, had originally had the experience when he was eighteen years old, but had never known what to make of it.) Paralleling the deepened relationship each of us was experiencing with the Lord, it seemed that as a family, too, we were becoming a closer, more tightly knit group than ever before.

As Madelyn would say, "The fruits of the Holy Spirit were everywhere evident."

Not only had Paulette's attitude been transformed to that of an enthusiastic, loving child of God; with straight A's at Ole Miss, she soon became a regular on the Dean's List. Heath, too, began to excel in his schoolwork; to Mother and Daddy's great joy, doctors and teachers alike agreed that it wouldn't be long before he would be completely caught up with other children his age. Tim and I, who had a history of getting along (or not getting along) like the Hatfields and McCoys, began to relate more like members of the same clan. And Mother and Daddy, well—often I caught them glancing at one another in the way it must have been like when they first started courting.

Our family's singing group, too, began to take off in new and exciting directions. Recent additions to The Prewitts were friends Cassandra Putnam, flutist, and Ralph Gordon, drummer. In demand more than ever, we began accepting out-of-state bookings, sometimes traveling to places as far away as Georgia, Arkansas, Tennessee, and Alabama.

It was a chilly evening in early spring and we were all assembled at a prayer meeting at Mamo's, when Madelyn cleared her throat as if to make an announcement.

"I've got something special to share," she said. "I've been waiting a long time for the right moment, and I do believe tonight's the night."

As I watched her reach into her handbag, I half expected her to pull out her pocket Bible. Instead, she withdrew a neatly folded sheet of white, lined paper.

"This," she said, as she carefully unfolded the paper and prepared to read, "is a covenant. It was written by Doyle Blackwood last summer, shortly before he died. He gave it to me to read once its contents had been fulfilled."

Doyle! At the mere mention of his name, my throat began to tighten, my eyes filled with tears. *How I missed him! If only he could know all the wonderful things that had taken place since his death*, I thought. *How happy he would be.*

"This covenant was written for some folks right here," continued Madelyn. "This covenant was written for the Prewitt family."

Shocked, I glanced at Mother and Daddy, who were as surprised at Madelyn's words as myself.

"This," Madelyn said, "is what Doyle wrote: 'I, Doyle Blackwood, do hereby make a covenant with my Lord, that the family of Hosea Amos Prewitt will come into the fullness of knowledge, love, and glory of His Holy Spirit; and that their gospel ministry will continue to grow and prosper and carry the good news of Jesus Christ throughout all Mississippi, and parts beyond.'

"After signing it," continued Madelyn, "Doyle sealed the covenant with his favorite scripture, Matthew 18:19: 'Again I say to you, if two of you agree on earth about anything they ask, it will be done for them by my Father in heaven.'

"This is one covenant," said Madelyn, as she handed the

sheet of paper to Daddy, "which I believe has been more than fulfilled. Don't you agree, Hosea?"

But Daddy, absorbed in examining the piece of paper, just nodded.

"Let me see," I said, rushing to his side. "Let me see what Doyle wrote." It was all I could do to stop myself from pulling the sheet out of Daddy's hand.

As I read over his shoulder, a chorus of questions cried out in my mind for answers: *How could Doyle have been so sure that all he had prayed for would come true? Was he aware, up in Heaven, of all that had happened? And what, exactly, was a covenant, anyway?*

Later, over coffee and carrot cake, some of my questions were answered. A covenant, I learned from Madelyn, is a simple, binding legal agreement between two parties. Probably the most famous covenants of all times were those made first by God with Abraham, in singling out the Jews as His chosen people and later by Jesus with all mankind, in enabling everyone—Jews and gentiles—access to God. Likewise today, explained Madelyn, we have the privilege of making covenants in faith between ourselves and God, as Doyle had done. This modern-day covenant making, I was surprised to learn, was common practice among many Christians.

"You know, Madelyn," I commented wistfully, "this is all so exciting and interesting—but isn't it too bad that Doyle couldn't be here to see his covenant prayers come true? It would have made him so happy."

"What do you mean, 'would have' made him happy?" asked Madelyn, seeming almost offended by my comment. "Knowing Doyle, I'm sure the act of simply making the covenant gave him as much joy and satisfaction as seeing it fulfilled."

"How can you say that?" I asked. "I don't understand."

"Honey," said Madelyn gently, "it's not that I don't miss Doyle and wish that he could be here, too. But faith is a mysterious and wonderful thing. According to the Bible, 'Now faith is the assurance of things hoped for, the conviction of things not seen' [Hebrews 11:1 RSV]. And that's exactly the kind of faith Doyle had. In Doyle's mind, you see, his prayers for your family had, from the moment he made them, already come true. That's why I'm certain that his joy in simply making the covenant was as deep — if not deeper — than it would be if he could be here this very moment."

"Well—" I said doubtfully, "that's a nice way for us to look at the situation. But I sure don't think I could ever claim that kind of faith for myself."

"I know you will," replied Madelyn, in a tone more prophetic than reassuring. "It's just a matter of time."

"BEAUTY PAGEANT?"

Rarely did Daddy raise his voice, but tonight his words fairly echoed throughout the house.

"No way." He shook his head stubbornly. "No way is a daughter of mine going to parade herself around in front of a bunch of strangers."

"But Daddy," I protested, "the judges aren't strangers; they're regular folks from Ackerman—just like us. And if I won, I'd be Miss Choctaw County!"

"Hmmph!" snorted Daddy, obviously unimpressed. "I don't rightly care if you were to become Miss America! I don't like the idea at all. Not one bit."

"Hosea," Mother interrupted gently, "if Cheryl were to win, there's a two-hundred-dollar cash prize she could use toward college. Becky Curtis says there's a good chance she can do it, too. Says she's got the talent—"

"Enough," said Daddy. "I've heard enough." He turned to regard me with penetrating eyes. "Young lady," he said solemnly, "you're eighteen years old now—grown enough to make your own decision about this matter. Therefore, I will not say no. But please know that as far as your participation in beauty pageants goes, I will not support you. Not now. Not ever. That's all I have to say."

With that, Daddy picked up his half-finished mug of coffee and left the supper table.

It was early spring, 1975, and I'd soon be finishing my senior year at Weir High. In the fall I was planning to attend Mississippi State University near Starkville, some thirty miles away, where I hoped to earn a double degree in voice and piano. To enter the Miss Choctaw County pageant, which was to take place in late March, had been Becky's idea.

"Cheryl," she had said to me some weeks earlier in the music room after school, "I think you know by now how gifted you are in music—not only in voice and piano, but in performing, too! The way I see it, there's an incredible future in store for you. But you're going to have to be willing to get out and go after it. I don't know exactly how to say this, Cheryl, but one of these days you're going to have to break away from Choctaw County, from Mississippi—maybe even from your family. Please don't get me wrong—it's just that I see so much *potential* in you. I mean, I just see so much *more* for you than a future spent teaching piano to kids and singing gospel music on the weekends. Do you understand what I'm trying to say?"

"Well," I had responded slowly, "I guess I haven't given the subject much thought. I do know I want to continue developing my talents to their fullest and using them to their best advantage. After all, that's what you've always encouraged me to do, and I think it's right."

"Good," said Becky. "Because the Miss Choctaw County pageant is coming up soon, and I think the experience would be good for you—good for your self-confidence and good for the exposure it would give you to different types of people and performing. I'm sure when you go away to college, you'll discover it's a whole new world there, too, and this might also help prepare you for that."

"I don't know," I said. "I mean, a beauty pageant—Mother might think the idea was kind of fun. But Daddy—I'm not so sure. I'll have to ask him and see what he says."

Now I had my answer. Daddy was dead set against my involvement in this, or any, pageant. Never had I gone against Daddy's will in any way, and now the mere thought of possibly doing so made me very unhappy. I felt torn, confused—as though my whole world had been turned inside out. Still, I wanted desperately to be in the pageant. I wanted to enter, and I wanted to win.

Carefully folding my napkin, I placed it by the side of my plate.

"Excuse me," I said, as I stood to leave the table. "I've got a phone call to make."

My heart was beating fast as I dialed Becky's number, but I tried to sound calm as I spoke.

"Becky?" I said, as I heard her answer. "It's me, Cheryl. I asked Daddy about being in the pageant, and though he did say he wouldn't support me, he didn't say no."

"Well?" asked Becky. "What are you going to do?"

"I'm going to enter," I said, hardly believing my own words. "I'm going to enter, and I'm going to do my best to win."

"Fabulous!" cried Becky. "Oh, Cheryl, it's going to be so much fun! Let's get together tomorrow afternoon after school and start making plans. There's lots to do, you know. Clothes to find, makeup to practice with, a whole talent routine to develop—"

"Great," I interrupted, as I heard Daddy coming down the hall. "See you tomorrow, then. Bye!"

"Who was that?" asked Daddy, as I quickly hung up the phone.

"Becky," I replied.

"You entering that contest?" he asked.

"Yes sir," I said, "I am."

His silence communicating his disapproval more eloquently than a thousand words, Daddy turned and continued down the hall.

Though I felt badly about going against his wishes, my feelings of remorse quickly vanished as I was caught up in the fun and excitement of preparing for the pageant. As Becky had said, it was, indeed, like entering a whole new world.

Sponsored by the Ackerman Lions Club, the pageant was to take place on the last Saturday of March in the Ackerman High gymnatorium (that's what they called their combination auditorium and gym). Thirteen girls would be competing for the title; most were college students, and as an eighteen-year-old high-schooler, I would be one of the youngest. Contestants would be judged in three categories: Talent, Swimsuit, and Evening Gown (or Poise and Personality). On the Friday before the event there would be a full dress rehearsal. Interviews by pageant judges would take place the following afternoon at Ackerman's city bank. On the night of the pageant, once the judges had selected the top five girls, the judging process would begin again with each category being worth equal percentage points. In addition to a $200 cash prize, the new Miss Choctaw County would be awarded assorted gifts from local merchants such as clothes, makeup, and gift certificates.

"The first thing we're going to have to do," said Becky on the following afternoon, "is get you some clothes."

"Clothes?" I asked. I glanced down at the navy blue A-line dress Mother had made for me. It was the same pattern as our sextet outfits had been that year. Whenever we had a new pattern, Mother always made the most of it. "What's the matter with my clothes?"

"Nothing's the matter," said Becky, "but when it comes to the pageant, you've got to look *outstanding*. We'll have to find you an evening gown, a Talent dress, a real smart-looking suit for your interview, and—"

"But Becky," I said, "you know I don't have that kind of money. All I've got saved is put away for college. I really shouldn't use it for anything else."

"No problem," said Becky. "We can borrow clothes. I've got a friend in Ackerman—you know her, Theresa McDonald, the high school music teacher—well, she's got a real cute red and white suit we can use for the interview. And for Talent, you can wear one of my halter-back dresses. Let's see —you're a size seven, right?"

"Right," I said.

"Shoes?" she asked.

"Seven," I said, slightly bewildered by all that was happening. "Same as you."

"Good!" said Becky. "You can wear my shoes, too."

"But Becky," I said a few moments later, "what about an evening gown? I don't know anybody who even owns one."

"Hm-m," said Becky, "that's a tough one. Guess we'll just have to ask around. We'll also have to find you a swimsuit."

"Swimsuit?" I cried. "But, Becky, I don't even know how to swim! I can't imagine what it's like to try a swimsuit on—let alone walk around in one."

"Don't worry," laughed Becky. "You'll learn. Come on, let's go to my place and look through my closet. I'll get you home in time for supper."

Later that evening, I told Paulette about our pageant preparations and how badly I needed to find an evening gown. "It needs to be something beautiful," I said. "Something elegant. Have any ideas?"

"Well," said Paulette thoughtfully, "why couldn't you use my old wedding gown? It's a nice off-white color and there's no lace. With a little work, it might be just what you need."

"Do you really think so?" I asked.

"Sure," she replied, "and I'll bet Mother would be glad to do it. Maybe she could ask Norma Snead to help—she's so good at sewing. About all they'd have to do is remove the train and size it to fit. Let's go ask Mother, and see what she says."

"Oh, Paulette," I cried. "*Thank you!* You don't know what this means to me!"

Less than a week later, Mother and Norma had fashioned from Paulette's old dress a lovely, long-sleeved, high-necked, velvet evening gown. It was, just as I had dreamed, elegant and beautiful.

Finding a swimsuit wasn't so easy.

After looking and looking in local shops, Becky and I finally had to carry our search to Columbus. Tall and thin, I was nearly impossible to fit; it took over three hours for us to find what we needed. A bright kelly green, the swimsuit featured a well-constructed top and ruffled neckline, which further served to camouflage my less-than-buxom chest. The swimsuit cost me $32.00. Matching green heels were $9.99. When I modeled the ensemble one evening for Mother in the music room, I thought she might faint. And when Tim and Heath accidentally entered the room their jaws dropped to nearly meet the floor.

"You're gonna wear that in public?" cried Tim, incredulously.

"Yes," I replied, in a voice sounding far more confident than I felt. "And I don't want to hear any more comments about it, thank you."

"I think it looks neat," grinned Heath. "I think you're gonna win."

"Well, one thing's for certain," I said, reaching down to ruffle his blond head. "I'm sure gonna try!"

Trying to maintain as much dignity as possible, I tottered across the uneven wooden floor over to the piano.

"Want to hear my Talent number?" I asked.

"Yeah!" cried Heath enthusiastically. "C'mon," he said, pulling at Tim's shirt sleeve, "let's sit down and listen. We can be Cheryl's audience."

My Talent number was an original routine conceived and developed by Becky and myself, which we'd come to refer to as "The Three B's." Traditionally, students of music recognize the "Three B's" as classical composers Bach, Beethoven, and Brahms. For our purposes, however, we strayed from tradition and changed Brahms to Bacharach, the well-known composer of many popular hits such as "Raindrops Keep Falling on My Head," "Do You Know the Way to San Jose?" "Walk on By," and many others. Within the three-minute routine, I sat at the piano and played and talked, offering the audience samples of the three different composers. Toward the end, I wrapped it up by saying, "But no matter what kind of music it is, I like it all, because . . ." And at that point I broke into singing the popular song "I Believe in Music," which, as a finishing touch, I played in the styles of each of the three different composers.

When I finished the number, Tim and Heath burst into spontaneous applause. Daddy, I noticed, was standing in the open doorway. He, however, was not applauding.

"What kind of music is that?" he asked.

"It's my pageant routine," I said. "It's what I'm going to perform in the Talent competition."

"You planning to sit at the piano wearing that getup?" he asked, referring to my swimsuit and heels.

"No sir," I said. "For Talent, I'll be wearing an evening gown. This is what I'll be wearing in the Swimsuit competition."

Again, as Daddy turned and left the room, his silence said more than a thousand words.

"Aw, don't feel bad," said Tim. "You know how Daddy is."

"I know," I said, "but it still bothers me."

As the weeks passed by and the pageant day drew near, more and more my doubts diminished and my desire to win grew. Every night I practiced for the pageant; I practiced walking in my swimsuit and evening gown, I rehearsed my Talent routine, I even brushed up on local Mississippi history, in case the judges asked some tricky questions. Never had I wanted to win anything so badly—not so much for the cash prize or the recognition, but simply for the sake of winning. To win the title of Miss Choctaw County was—like so many goals Becky had set before me over the years—just another objective to be met. Once accomplished, I'd then go on to set my sights on something else.

It therefore came as something of a shock, when, during the Friday night rehearsal prior to the pageant, I discovered that not all contestants shared my shortsighted outlook. One of the girls, a pretty blonde named Cathy Cooper, was a senior at Mississippi University for Women majoring in music. Her long-range goal, should she win the title of Miss Choctaw County, was to go on to compete in the Miss Mississippi pageant in Vicksburg.

"Can you believe it?" I said to Becky, when we met after the rehearsal. "I had no idea this had anything to do with the Miss Mississippi pageant. I thought it ended right here with Miss Choctaw County."

"Oh, no," said Becky. "For a lot of girls this represents a first step toward being Miss America! This is what's known as an official local pageant; all over the country they're taking place this time of year. Winners of locals will then compete in the summer for state titles—there are usually forty or fifty girls in those competitions—and then those state winners are the ones who will go on to try for Miss America in September. I didn't realize you weren't aware of this."

"No," I said, shaking my head. "I wasn't. Not at all. And you know what, Becky?"

"What?"

"It makes me want to win all the more."

"Well," said Becky, "wanting to win can't hurt. Tomorrow night will tell the story."

On the afternoon of the pageant I was so excited I could hardly fasten the buttons on my borrowed red and white suit. Becky picked me up at 2:00 P.M., to take me to the judges' interview which would take place in the president's office of Ackerman's city bank.

"Now remember," whispered Becky, as she walked me into the building, "be yourself. And don't forget to smile!"

"Will do," I said, stooping to check my hair in the reflection of the bank's silver water fountain. "See you soon."

As I heard one of the pageant officials call my name and I stood to enter the interview room, I felt almost giddy. Waiting for me were five judges: local Lions Club members and Ackerman civic and business leaders. As I sat down, I remembered to cross my legs at the ankles as Becky had instructed me. I smiled.

"Well now, Miss Prewitt," said one of the judges, "where do you come from?"

"Oh," I said lightly, "I live in the country."

"Country?" asked the judge. "What, exactly, do you classify as country?"

"Why, I live so far out in the country," I said, recalling one of Pa Prewitt's favorite expressions, "they have to pump the sunshine in!"

The judge, glancing at one of his colleagues, began to laugh. I laughed, too.

"Tell me," said another judge, "who is William Winter?"

"William Winter?" I repeated, "I'm not sure. Doesn't he have something to do with politics?"

"You might say that," said the judge, pursing his lips in an effort not to laugh. "He's our lieutenant governor."

"Oh!" I cried. "I had no idea!"

"Well now," said another judge, a formidable-looking woman in black, "what exactly do you think about the swimsuit competition? Some people feel it's demeaning to women, you know."

"Not me!" I said. "I think it's great! I mean, you wouldn't want Miss Choctaw County to be some girl with great gobs of fat hanging all over her body, now would you? What better way is there to find out what's really there, other than putting her in a swimsuit?"

This time, all the judges laughed—including the woman who had asked the question. In fact, everyone seemed to be having such an uproariously good time that I thought it best to join in the fun by slapping my knee and laughing right along with them.

Later, when I told Becky about my interview, she didn't think it was funny at all.

"Cheryl!" she cried. "You weren't supposed to be a comedian. You were supposed to be sophisticated. Poise and personality, remember? That's what the judges were looking for."

"Sophisticated?" I said. "Why didn't you tell me? Shoot, now I'll never win."

"Well," said Becky, "you never can tell how judges figure. Maybe they liked you for your candor. You know, natural charm and all that."

"Oh well," I said, "at least they had a good time."

That afternoon I stayed at Becky's until it was time to pack the car with my dresses, shoes, and swimsuit and head for the Ackerman gymnatorium. A member of the Ackerman Lions Club, Becky's husband, Robert, went along, too. Arriving at the same time as we did was Theresa McDonald. With Becky, she would be providing the evening's background music at the piano.

Once backstage and dressed in my evening gown for my initial walk across the stage, I peeked through the curtain and picked out Mother, Paulette, Aunt Dot, Uncle James, and various other kin in the audience. Daddy was not there. For a moment I felt a pang of remorse at his absence—but that quickly passed in the thrill of the competition.

Never had I felt so wonderful. Walking in my evening gown, I felt as though I were a queen, floating on air. In my swimsuit, too, I felt confident and mature. And when it came time to do my Talent routine, never had I put so much effort into a performance. I could tell by the audience's warm response that they had enjoyed listening to "The Three B's" as much as I had enjoyed performing it.

Later, when I heard my name announced as one of the top five contestants, I was almost not surprised. I'd felt so good throughout the entire evening. But when the five of us made our final walk across the stage and gathered backstage for the final judging, I felt my emotions swelling to proportions almost too big for me to handle.

What if I won? I thought. *What if I went to Vicksburg to try for the title of Miss Mississippi? What if—oh please, God,* I prayed silently, *let me win!*

My prayer was interrupted as I heard the emcee begin to announce the winners' names, from the bottom, up.

"Fourth runner-up, third runner-up, second runner-up . . ."

Suddenly, there I was, standing backstage with Cathy Cooper. One of us would be the next Miss Choctaw County.

"Oh, Cathy," I said, grabbing hold of her hand and squeezing it, "isn't this exciting?"

Cathy, however, was unresponsive—intent upon hearing the emcee's next words.

"First runner-up," he began—and then stopped. "Before announcing the first runner-up," he said, "perhaps I should explain the importance of this position."

The audience groaned at the delay.

Reveling in his captive crowd, the emcee continued.

"Should Miss Choctaw County for some reason be unable to fulfill her duties," he explained, "her title would then be transferred to the first runner-up. And that person, first runner-up for Miss Choctaw County, is . . . Miss Cheryl Prewitt!"

Me! I had won! Or, I had almost won. Whatever it was I had done, I cried with excitement as I walked onstage and accepted the chrome and plastic trophy that was the first runner-up's award. Then my moment in the spotlight quickly faded in light of the attention and praise being shone upon Cathy Cooper, the new Miss Choctaw County.

While thrilled beyond words for my achievement, at the same time I felt as though I had fallen short of my goal. Cathy had won. Cathy would be going to Vicksburg to compete in the Miss Mississippi pageant. I had done well, but Cathy had done better.

The experience reminded me of the first piano recital Becky had urged me to compete in. I was in the ninth grade and returned home having achieved only "Excellent," when the top rank had been "Superior." Likewise, tonight, I had wanted desperately to be the best, but had been only second best. To my mind, therefore, I had lost altogether.

And what, I wondered vaguely, as I gathered my clothes and makeup, *had become of my prayer? Where had God been when I had needed Him?*

Later, when I shared my thoughts with Becky in the car on the way home, she was quiet for a long while. Finally, she spoke.

"Cheryl," she said, "after listening to you talk, it occurs to me that there are three good lessons we can learn from your experience tonight. And though it may sound funny—in one way or another, they all have to do with God."

"Tell me," I said.

"First," said Becky, "I think it's important to realize that in any competition, the only person you can honestly compete with is yourself. The moment you start worrying about other people—how good or bad they are compared to your-self—jealousy or pride are sure to creep in to distract you. And jealousy and pride are not feelings God wants us to have —anytime.

"It seems to me that all we're called to do—no matter what the competition—is the best we can. We have to learn to measure our efforts not against other people, but against our-selves, our yardstick being our past performance and known potential."

"Makes sense," I said. "What else?"

"Second," said Becky, "I think it's important to realize the silliness of panic prayers; you know, like tonight when you said, 'Please God, let me win.' "

"Yeah," I grinned sheepishly. "My motivation wasn't exactly what you'd call pure, was it?"

"No," laughed Becky, "it sure wasn't. And you, Cheryl Prewitt, know as well as anyone how God searches our hearts and knows us inside out. Besides, it's my opinion that no matter how much faith we have in a given outcome to a situation, all the faith in the world can't override God's will. And I just really believe, Cheryl, deep down in my spirit, that it was God's will you didn't win tonight—that He wanted you to be first runner-up."

"But why?" I asked. "I tried so hard. I did everything I could. I know I did my absolute best—and still I didn't win."

"That brings me to my third point," said Becky. "As Christians, I think that ultimately we have to learn to trust God's promise in Romans 8:28: 'All things work together for good to them that love God' [King James Version]. *All* things, He says. Not just some. Not just those things that makes us happy. We may not know why you didn't win the title of Miss Choctaw County tonight, but God does. What we can know is that what He wants for you is for you to be right where you are this moment—first runner-up, with a fabulous introduction to pageants and a wonderful college career to look forward to."

"I guess you're right," I sighed. "It was a wonderful experience. I'm glad I did it."

By the time Becky dropped me off at the door, my spirits were considerably improved. Anxious to talk to Daddy, I ran into the living room where he was settled in his easy chair reading his Bible.

"Daddy!" I cried, "I won! Well—I almost won. That is, I came in first runner-up."

"Well," said Daddy dryly, not bothering to turn his eyes from the opened book, "why didn't you win the title?"

Frustrated by Daddy's response, I fumbled for words. "Well," I said, "I will. Next time, I will!"

IF PARTICIPATING in the Miss Choctaw County pageant had seemed like entering a whole new world, then enrolling as a freshman at Mississippi State University was like being transported to a different galaxy.

With a student population exceeding thirteen thousand and a lush rolling six hundred fifty–acre campus, MSU was a city unto itself—complete with its own tree-lined streets, housing, shops, cinema, theater, stadium, newspaper, and zip code. When I first arrived it seemed I wanted to become involved in everything—from student government to on-campus church groups. But I quickly discovered that with my heavier than normal work load, such involvement would not be possible.

Working toward a double major in music education (piano and voice), I would be averaging between eighteen and twenty-four hours of classes each semester, not including two to three practice hours each day. The Music Department (where I spent most of my time) was small but thriving. Competition among students, though rarely talked about, was stiff. Fortunately, at Becky's urging earlier in the year, I had applied and qualified for the position of accompanist for the school's Choir and Madrigal Singers—a job that not only enabled me to gain extra experience and travel, but also fostered a close relationship between myself and Jerry Williams, MSU's choral director. In addition, the position earned me an extra $88.00 a month—and when it came to finances, every little bit helped. I also sold cosmetics and continued teaching piano and voice at home on weekends.

I guess I'd been at school for about a month when I realized that my lifestyle (though I was registered as a full-time student and resident) was more like that of a commuter, or day student. While I remained on campus during the week, Friday afternoons found me hopping into my 1969 Plymouth (the "Green Machine" I called it) and returning home for weekends of teaching, selling cosmetics, and singing with the family. Rarely did I return to campus before Monday morning.

Often I wished I could stay at school full time, but despite my weekend absences I still felt very much a part of MSU's student body. Such feelings of belonging were largely due not only to my close relationships with teachers and friends in the Music Department—but to the deep friendship I shared with my roommate, Pam Williams.

Pam and I first met in September 1974, when my family performed during a weekend retreat at Rabbit Ridge, a Christian summer camp in northern Mississippi. Coincidentally, it was Doyle and Lavez Blackwood who brought us together; Pam was from Byhalia, Mississippi, a small town not too far from Memphis. Like myself, Pam had been praying for months to find a roommate for her upcoming year at MSU; like Mother and Daddy, her folks had been reluctant to have her leave home without knowing in advance who that person would be. We were, therefore, thrilled upon meeting each other. And with Pam's sweet nature, not to mention her obvious love for the Lord, the two of us hit it off immediately.

From outward appearances, it might seem that Pam and I had little in common: Pam was petite and blonde; I was tall and brunette. Pam was an only child; I was from a large family. Pam was a pragmatically minded math major; I was a more emotionally bent musician. Moreover, Pam was a meticulous housekeeper, while wherever I passed seemed to take on the appearance of a disaster area! Both of us, however, were Christians—and it was through this simple spiritual bond that we struck a common cord. Because of our shared faith, all seeming differences dissolved.

As freshmen, we were assigned to Cresswall Hall, one of the larger dormitories on campus. Over the summer Pam had suggested that we decorate our room in shades of blue, and she had purchased matching bedspreads and contact paper for our bookshelves. She also bought a small refrigerator, for which Daddy constructed a matching cabinet which also served as the shelf for the rest of our "kitchen"—a hot plate, toaster oven, popcorn popper, and Crock-Pot.

First on our agenda in decorating the room was covering its bleak cement-block walls with a riot of posters—most with Christian themes. One such poster showed a misty photo of a young girl gazing out an open window with a large caption reading, "I'm afraid of tomorrow." Below, in smaller print, and noted with a small white cross, were the words (Jesus' reply), "Don't worry, I've already been there." Another poster featured a brilliant close-up of a wild flower with the large caption exclaiming, "Wow, that's beautiful!" In smaller print below—again marked with a small white cross—was the reply, "Thanks, I made it!"

"Bless this room, Father," Pam and I prayed our first night together. "Fill it with Your peace, and make it a place where You are always present. Help us to be good witnesses for You during our years at MSU. Use us to bring others to know Your power and love. In Jesus' name we pray—amen."

It was a simple prayer. Spontaneous, too. But as a result, Pam and I noticed that two things began to happen. First, from that day on, not an evening passed when we didn't take time to pray together; even when one of us had a date or late night at the library, that person always made a special point to wake the other for a quick word with the Lord before going to bed. Second, it seemed that other girls on the floor began to gravitate to our room—often with no other intention than to say hello and chat.

"It just feels so good in here," they'd often say. "I don't know exactly how to describe it, but it sure is different. Somehow—peaceful."

When this happened, Pam and I would wink at each other.

Without a doubt, the most frequent visitors to our room were our next-door neighbors, Lori and Margaret. Like ourselves, both girls were from Mississippi and had been raised in Christian homes. Lori, slim and outspoken with a dazzling smile, was also a music major who shared many classes with me. Margaret was the quieter of the two. A natural beauty with smoky eyes and shoulder length dark hair, she was still undecided about her major.

During our first few weeks as freshmen, it seemed that Lori and Margaret were always visiting; the four of us spent endless hours talking, laughing, and consuming substantial amounts of popcorn and diet soda. By October, however, the girls' visits had considerably lessened—especially those made by Margaret. Often we wondered why.

One Thursday evening, when Pam and I were studying, we heard a tentative rap on the door. It was Lori.

"Hi, y'all," she said, peering around the half-opened door. "Hope I'm not disturbing you. Do you think we could talk for a minute?"

Her face was drawn and anxious. Gone was the dazzling smile.

"Sure," I said. "Come on in. There's nothing wrong, is there?"

"Well," said Lori, "I'm all right—but I'm worried about Margaret. I guess you-all know she's picked up smoking since she came to school. And that's not so bad. But recently she's started drinking, too. You know, on dates and at parties."

"Drinking?" I asked incredulously. "Margaret?"

"It's not that bad," said Lori. "I mean, it's not like she goes out and gets drunk or anything. And I know the only reason she's doing it is because everyone else is. What worries me is the possibility that she might go on to try more serious things—like marijuana, or other drugs."

"Not that bad!" I cried. "I had no idea those kinds of

things were going on around here—especially drugs." I turned to face Pam. "Is that true?"

"Sure," replied Pam, apparently surprised by my reaction. "But it's the same stuff that goes on at any college. Nothing unusual."

"But *drugs*," I repeated. Even the word sounded ugly.

"Cheryl," said Pam quietly, "there are a lot of things that go on around here—mostly over weekends. But you're so rarely here; that's why I think it comes as such a surprise to you."

"Oh," I said lamely. "I see." Actually, I was stunned.

"Hey you two," interrupted Lori. "What about Margaret? Do you have any ideas how we might be able to help her? I'd hate to see her suddenly find herself in a situation too big to handle."

"Well," said Pam thoughtfully, "why don't we confront her with our concern face to face. You know, as friends."

"I don't know," replied Lori. "She's been awfully moody lately. And the few times I've mentioned the subject, she's really gotten mad."

"Where is she now?" asked Pam.

"Next door," said Lori. "I'm afraid she knows we're talking about her."

"In that case," said Pam, "I definitely think we should speak to her." She turned to face me. "What do you think, Cheryl?"

"Don't see how it could hurt," I said. "Now's as good a time as ever."

When Margaret arrived, however, I wondered if we might have made a mistake. Clearly annoyed, she carried in one hand her cigarettes and lighter—in the other, an empty Coke can for an ashtray.

"What's going on here?" she asked. "What, exactly, is the problem?"

"Sit down," said Pam softly. "We just wanted to talk, that's all."

"What about?" said Margaret, perching on the edge of my bed. She set her Coke can on the floor. "My smoking?"

"No," said Pam. "Your drinking."

"My drinking?" cried Margaret, with a derisive laugh. "You make me sound like I'm an alcoholic or something." She glared at Lori. "What have you been telling them about me?"

"Only the truth," replied Lori. "That you've taken up with a crowd that drinks—and that it's got me worried. Besides, it's just not right. As believers, we aren't supposed to do that sort of thing."

"Listen," said Margaret, "I'm just as good a Christian now as I ever was—whether or not I drink or smoke makes no difference. I believe in Jesus just the same as I always have."

"*We* know that," said Pam, "but what about the effect your behavior has on people who aren't Christians—people who look to you as an example? If your life as a believer differs from theirs in no discernible way—then why should they bother becoming one at all? It's just not a good witness."

"Besides," I added, "it's dangerous, spiritually—like treading on thin ice as far as God is concerned."

"How so?" asked Margaret.

"Well," I said, "once you alter your consciousness just the tiniest bit, you open yourself up to all kinds of evil influences; for example, your sense of discernment between good and evil and your ability to resist temptations are lessened across the board. Satan just loves it when that happens. And there are some folks who believe that addictions such as alcoholism, gluttony, and gambling and chronically negative states of mind such as envy, bitterness, and depression are more than learned patterns of behavior—they're actually bad spirits. As such, if you repeatedly let your guard down, they can literally enter, take up residence in you, and wreak havoc with your life."

"What?" cried Margaret. "Do you mean to tell me you really believe that stuff? You really believe in Satan and his demons?"

For a moment the silence in the room was so thick, I thought it might never be broken. Finally, however, I spoke.

"Well yes, Margaret," I said. "Yes, I do."

"You've got to be kidding!" she cried. Whirling around, she turned to face Pam. "What about you?"

"Well," replied Pam, "I've got to agree with Cheryl. If you're going to believe in Jesus, then you've got to believe in Satan." Reaching over to her nightstand, she picked up her Bible. "It's all right here, you know. Hard to deny."

"Honestly!" cried Margaret. "You guys are too much. First you try to tell me there's something wrong with me because I occasionally take a drink. Then you try to tell me I'd better watch out, or the devil's gonna get me. Well, if you want to know the truth, I think you're all a bunch of simple-minded fundamentalists—not to mention crazy. Thanks for your concern, friends—but next time I want some advice, I'll ask for it."

Her dark eyes flashing with anger, Margaret stormed out of the room, slamming the door behind her. For the first time since our arrival at Cresswall Hall, the peace in our little room had been decidedly shattered.

A few moments later, the three of us heard the squeak of a hinge as Margaret opened the next-door window.

"She's having a cigarette," explained Lori. "She always opens the window when she smokes."

Still shaken by the interlude, Pam and I said nothing.

"I'm sorry," said Lori. "Sorry this had to happen. I think I'd better go now." Sighing, she stood and walked to the door. "Pray for us," she said before leaving. "Okay?"

"Sure," said Pam. "You bet."

In silence, the two of us returned to our studies—though it was clear after just a few minutes of reading that we were too upset to accomplish anything.

"Let's just go to bed and get up early," I suggested. "Maybe then we'll feel more like studying."

"Good idea," said Pam, closing her book. "I'm exhausted."

Before going to bed, Pam walked across the room to open our window. The night was unusually warm for October, and Pam liked the fresh air.

"One of these days," she said while climbing into bed, "we've got to get a shade for that window. That street lamp's brighter than a full moon."

"Yeah," I murmured absently, "one of these days we'll have to do that."

As was our habit, we held hands above the small chasm between our twin beds and said a short prayer, tonight making sure to mention Lori and Margaret. Then I watched as Pam rolled over and promptly fell asleep.

Still upset, I tried to relax by watching the moving shadows of branches and leaves that covered our ceiling and walls. The shadows were caused by the street lamp shining through the trees outside the window.

I must have been staring at the shadows for a good five minutes when suddenly, as though blotted out by a huge dark hand, the patterns lost all definition. For a moment I thought the street lamp must have gone out. But as seconds passed and the room continued to grow increasingly dark, I realized that it had to be something else.

But what?

"Pam?" I whispered fearfully. But asleep, she didn't hear me.

At once I was gripped with terror like I'd never known as the darkness—almost like a presence—closed in to fill the space between myself and the ceiling! In a matter of seconds, everything was black. It was as though I was lost, adrift in a sea of darkness, when suddenly—horribly—I felt the foot of my bed being raised off the floor! Noiselessly, effortlessly, as though by the same invisible force that had darkened the room, my bed continued to rise until my feet were well above my head. Paralyzed with fear, it was all I could do to cry out.

"*Pam!*"

"Huh?" she answered, still groggy with sleep.

"Something's wrong," I said. "Something's terribly wrong. Oh, Pam—I'm so scared!"

"What is it?" she asked, now fully awake.

"My bed," I said. "Someone is lifting my bed! Look!"

I listened to the rustle of sheets as Pam sat up.

"Cheryl," she gasped, "where are you? I can't see you anywhere. Everything's so black! Oh, Cheryl, what's happening?"

I heard the sound of her feet touching the floor.

"I'm turning on the light," she said.

"No!" I cried.

Suddenly, as if frightened by the threat of disclosure, the darkness dissipated. Without a sound, my bed dropped to the floor. Again, the room was flooded with light from the street lamp.

Pam was about halfway to the light switch when I noticed a dark circular spot in the corner of the room, near the window. It looked as though someone had spilled black ink on the floor. The area, which measured about two feet across, was blacker than anything I'd ever seen. It almost seemed to have its own depth and dimension—as though it might be an entranceway to some bottomless pit. Horrified, I realized that it was the same blackness that had enveloped me when my bed had been lifted off the floor.

"Pam!" I cried. "Stop! Don't move!"

"Why?" she asked.

"Look!" I pointed. "That spot—over there on the floor by the window."

Transfixed by the blackness, Pam froze in her tracks.

"What is it?" she asked in a hushed tone.

"I don't know," I said. "But it's bad. It's evil. And—and—in the name of Jesus, I rebuke its presence in our room!"

"I'm turning on the light," said Pam.

Flying to the side of the room, she flicked the switch.

The spot was gone.

Exhausted by the ordeal, I collapsed into tears.

"Cheryl," said Pam consolingly, "it's all over. It's gonna be all right." Climbing onto my bed, she wrapped her arms around me. "But tell me, what happened? What was it?"

Still shaking, I related my experience.

"Weird," she commented when I told her about my bed being raised. "Really scary."

She nodded in agreement as I described the horrible blackness and the spot on the floor.

"Pam," I said, when I had finished, "I can't tell you how scared I am. Please pray with me. Please pray till I get a peace about this whole thing. It's really got me rattled. I mean, I've never been so frightened."

"Of course," she replied. "It's got me pretty uptight, too."

So for four solid hours Pam and I prayed, together asking God to bless and protect us and to restore peace and tranquillity to our room. It was 3:00 A.M. when we finally turned out the light. Even then, I could not sleep.

Over and over, recollections of the eerie darkness, the sensation of my bed being lifted, and the lingering spot returned to haunt me. But no matter how I tried, I could make no sense of the experience. All I knew was that it had been bad—the very essence of evil—and very, very threatening.

A few mornings later, I was seated at my makeup mirror applying eyeliner, when Pam—cup of coffee in one hand, her

Bible in the other—came over and sat down in the empty chair next to me.

"You know, Cheryl," she said, "I've been doing a lot of thinking about what happened the other night, and I think I might have an answer, or at least a theory."

"What's that?" I asked, a chill running down my spine at the mere mention of the incident.

"Well," she said, setting her Bible on the desk, and stirring her coffee slowly, "I think we were visited by a bad spirit."

"A what?" I asked.

"A bad spirit," she repeated. "You know, one of Satan's cohorts—like the kind we were talking about the other night. I also think it might have been the same spirit that's lately been bothering Margaret."

Fascinated at Pam's idea, I put down my eyeliner brush and turned to face her. "You mean the spirit that's been urging her to smoke and drink?" I asked.

"That's right," said Pam. "Remember how when she left our room, we heard her open her window to smoke a cigarette? Well, our window was open, too, and I think that old spirit—annoyed at our accusations and interference—decided to come over and pay us a visit. You know, to shake us up a little bit.

"Look here," she continued, reaching for her Bible, which was fairly stuffed with reference markers, "I've been doing some reading on the subject, and it all makes sense. There's nothing, you see, that makes life easier for Satan than those people who don't believe in him. It's the believers who give him a real headache. The way I understand it, Satan's sole function—aided by his demons—is to mar God's creation and destroy God's people. That's why, as Christians, we have to be especially alert to his wily ways. While he may sometimes choose to reveal himself in all his frightful wickedness—as he did to us—he's equally able to transform himself into an 'angel of light,' should that better suit his purpose [2 Corinthians 11:14]."

"Maybe that's the approach he's taking with Margaret," I said. "You know, by making smoking and drinking seem appealing for the sophistication and freedom they seem to symbolize, when actually both—when carried to extremes—are crippling forms of bondage."

"Exactly," said Pam. "Satan's means to catastrophic ends are often subtle. The Bible's full of examples — and warnings. Peter said it well when he advised, 'Be sober, be watchful. Your adversary the devil prowls around like a roaring lion, seeking some one to devour' [I Peter 5:8 RSV]. Paul mentions in his letter to the church at Thessalonica, how the devil hindered his missionary efforts [I Thessalonians 2:18] and in his first letter to Timothy goes so far as to suggest that it's the devil's special delight to deceive, if possible, the very leaders of the church [I Timothy 3:6]! Margaret's such a good kid — no wonder he's got his eye on her!"

Suddenly, our conversation was interrupted by a knock at the door.

"Door's open," I called. "Come on in."

Pam and I both blinked with surprise to see that our visitor was none other than Margaret.

"Hi, you guys," she said. "Hope I'm not interrupting anything. Mind if I come in?"

"Not at all," said Pam. "Fact is, we were just talking about you."

"Well," said Margaret in a low voice, "I can't blame you." She sat on my bed. "I just wanted to say I'm sorry about the other night. I really don't know what got into me, but I'm feeling a lot better now. I've been thinking about what you-all said—you know, about smoking and drinking—and I realize you're right. I'm thinking twice now before doing either one. It's really made a difference."

"Oh, Margaret," I said, "that's so good to hear."

"You know," she went on, "I've also been thinking about what you-all said about the devil. When I recall the way my behavior's been these past few weeks—especially the way I flared up at you the other night—it's scary. Almost as though it hasn't really been me. And that night when I left your room, I can't begin to describe how horrible I felt—so dark, depressed, and angry. Really ugly. After smoking a cigarette, I went right to bed. I was that anxious to get away from my feelings."

"Really?" I asked. "We had a pretty rough time of it that night, too."

"How so?" asked Margaret.

"Well," I began, glancing over at Pam, who was nodding eagerly as if to say, *Go on, tell her.* "It all started after we went to bed . . ."

"Wow," Margaret commented, after listening to our experience and Pam's theory with wide-eyed interest. "That's spooky. Sure does make you wonder, doesn't it?"

"Yes," I said. "Pam and I were just talking about it when you came in."

"I was just getting to the good part," said Pam, opening her Bible. "Mind if I continue?"

"Please do," grinned Margaret.

"Well," said Pam, "the good news is that Satan—for all his seeming clever ways and frantic activity—is, in the light of God, a pathetic wretch, ultimately doomed to failure. In fact, it was for this reason that God sent Jesus into the world—that the works of the devil, including death, might be destroyed [1 John 3:8]. In the eternal scheme of things, you see, Satan is already defeated. As Christians, therefore, all we have to do is detect and resist him—just as we did the other night—and he will flee [James 4:7]. That's God's promise to us. And believe me, God never lies."

For a moment the three of us fell silent, each considering

the ramifications of what had been said, when suddenly, in a small voice, Margaret spoke up.

"Want to pray?" she asked.

"Sure," said Pam.

The three of us held hands as she led the prayer.

"Thank You, Father," she said, "for this experience which has served to remind us not only of Satan's reality and power in this world, but, moreover, of Your all-powerful love and concern for us, Your children, in sending Your only son, Jesus, to die for us. Protect us, Father, and give us discerning hearts so that we may detect Satan the next time he comes around to bother us. Give us also the strength and will to resist him so that he can't so much as touch us. Thanks also for our friendship, and for the ability to talk to You this way in prayer. In Jesus' name we pray—amen."

"O-oh," I said, upon opening my eyes, "that felt so good."

Having prayed, it was as though the peace in our room had at last been fully and completely restored.

When Margaret had gone, Pam and I continued to talk about all that had happened.

"You know," I said, "two things strike me as a result of this experience."

"What?" asked Pam.

"Well," I said, "the first is obvious, and that's a new realization and understanding of old Satan's nature and doings here on earth. It's the second item that's got me puzzled. Pam —I don't know exactly how to say this—but I've got this burning desire to go out and start warning people to be careful, to tell them about God's love, and Jesus, and the Holy Spirit, and to encourage them to at least consider trying Christianity."

"Gosh," said Pam, "you sound like a missionary."

"I know," I said. "And that's what has me worried. The kind of witnessing I want to do is on a scale far larger than anything possible now—even considering all the performing I do with my family. The problem is, I'm happy with my life the way it is. I'm happy here at MSU. I don't want to go to Africa or China as some missionary." Pausing, I frowned. "What if God wants me to go to Africa or China?"

"Cheryl," laughed Pam, "*relax*. God doesn't work that way. If He wanted you to pack your bags and Bible and set sail for China, then that's the desire He'd place in your heart. It must be something else He's got planned for you—so don't worry. All He wants us to do is love Him, be obedient to Him, keep the lines of communication open through prayer— and He promises to bring us into His perfect will more gracefully than we could ever do ourselves. One thing's for sure, Cheryl: God won't be calling you anywhere until you're ready to go."

"Well that's good to hear," I said. "Because I've got the strangest feeling that wherever it is He wants me to go and whatever it is He wants me to do, it's gonna take a lot of preparation."

"Could be," said Pam. "That wouldn't surprise me a bit."

IT WAS JANUARY 1978, the last semester of my junior year, and I was walking through the student union building on my way to the school bookstore.

Suddenly, from the corner of my eye, I glimpsed an all-too-familiar face smiling from a poster on the campus bulletin board. There, in all her regal splendor, was this year's Miss Mississippi State University, Patti Walton—her smiling face a reminder to all who passed by to support the school's basketball team. For me, however, the poster served as a reminder of something much more personal: tryouts for next year's new Miss MSU were just around the corner.

The Miss MSU pageant, a two-day competition which took place in the school's huge auditorium in late March, was traditionally one of the most popular events on campus. Qualifying as a Miss America local, the pageant had a reputation as being among the state's toughest. Indeed, in past years, many a Miss MSU had gone on to Vicksburg to become Miss Mississippi and, in September, to Atlantic City to compete for the title of Miss America. Regardless of subsequent successes, Miss MSU was guaranteed a year-long reign as official representative for one of the South's best-known schools—not to mention a $500 cash award.

Last year's pageant winner, Patti Walton (Miss MSU for the 1977–78 school year), was, like myself, a music major from Choctaw County. Now, as I regarded her smiling face, nagging feelings of disappointment and discontent churned inside me. For the past two years I'd competed for the title of Miss MSU—and lost. When I'd entered for the first time as a freshman and finished as second runner-up, it hadn't been too bad; after all, most of the finalists were upperclassmen. Last year's experience, however, had been devastating. Entering the pageant as a sophomore with the specific aim to win, I'd finished as third runner-up.

Third! It had been a crushing blow—not only for me, but for Becky and Pam and everyone else who had come to see me win. Fortunately, in the encounters immediately following the pageant, I'd somehow managed to maintain a reasonable facade of gracious good cheer: "Oh, gee," I smiled, in reply to those who expressed sorrow at my loss. "I'm just thrilled to have made it as a finalist."

Alone with Pam, however, the truth exploded: "Never!" I vowed, between racking sobs, "never am I ever entering another pageant!"

"There, there," Pam had replied. "Don't cry." Like a mother doing her best to soothe a hopelessly disconsolate infant, she patted me reassuringly on the shoulder. For half the night, we drove around Starkville in her car—hashing and rehashing the details of the pageant, trying to figure out why I had fared so poorly.

"Well," Pam had concluded by the time we pulled into the dormitory parking lot, "there's obviously some good reason you didn't win. We just don't know what it is, that's all."

"I'll tell you what's obvious," I had said glumly. "It's obvious that I'm washed up."

A few days later—after listening to lots of Mozart and doing my best to recall Becky's long-ago shared words of wisdom about competing and losing—I finally was able to surrender the problem to God in prayer and felt a lot better. Still, judging by my reaction to Patti Walton's poster, it was apparent that my wounded pride had not yet fully recovered.

Sighing, I turned from the bulletin board and continued on toward the bookstore. Today was Thursday, and tomorrow I'd be heading home for the weekend. Some of my more advanced piano students had recently expressed interest in learning about music composition, and I needed to buy a few extra tablets of scoring paper.

While standing in the check-out line, my thoughts turned

again to the upcoming Miss MSU competition. *How won-derful it must be*, I thought dreamily, *to serve as official representative for such a fabulous school . . .*

If anything, my freshman infatuation with MSU had, over the years, matured to a deep, abiding love. My relationship with the Music Department continued to be especially rewarding; as accompanist and soloist with the MSU Choir and Madrigal Singers, I'd also appeared as concert pianist for the Jackson Symphony Orchestra and as vocal soloist for the Starkville Symphony. Though it sometimes was a struggle, my grades were good; a President's List Scholar, I'd also (much to Mother's and Daddy's delight) been listed in *Who's Who in American Colleges and Universities*. Socially, also, I'd fared pretty well; though I wasn't around on weekends, I had many girl friends, and the boys seemed to like me all right, too. In my freshman year, I'd been named a Little Sister for Phi Mu Alpha fraternity and later as a Sweetheart for Phi Gamma Delta. It was, in fact, the brothers of Phi Gamma Delta who repeatedly sponsored my participation in campus pageants.

Ah, pageants.

Like my fondness for school, my passion for pageants had also, over the years, continued to grow. I absolutely loved the challenge of competing. The thrill of performing. About the only thing I didn't like was losing. That, however, hadn't been a serious problem until the past year.

If only, I thought wistfully, *I could combine my love for pageants and for my school and somehow win the title of Miss MSU . . . What better way to spend my senior year? Still, to return to the pageant for a third time would be so embarrassing. And what if, for all my efforts, I were again to lose?* I shuddered at the thought.

Still, unable to forget the idea, I mentioned the subject to Becky the following Saturday morning. Sitting in the music room we talked while awaiting the arrival of my next student, ten-year-old Sammy Wood, Madelyn and Web's little boy.

"Shoot," I exclaimed, after sharing my thoughts about the pageant. "I wish I'd never seen that old poster."

"Why?" asked Becky. "Maybe you should enter."

"What?" I cried. "And risk humiliating myself again? No thanks."

"Well," said Becky, "I think you should at least consider it. If you want my honest opinion, I think you could win. You're the best girl around, you know. You've got the talent. You've got the looks. You've got the personality—"

"Stop!" I cried. "Stop this minute, Becky Curtis! You know how that kind of talk affects me; I'm so dad-gummed goal-oriented, it's like dangling a carrot in front of a horse. I got this way thanks to you, I might add."

Our conversation was interrupted by the sound of a car pulling into the front drive. It was Madelyn and Sammy. Sammy was one of my favorite students. Often I laughed with amusement at the fact of our three-generation span as teachers—Madelyn had taught Becky, Becky had taught me, and now I was teaching Sammy. Today, however, I had other things on my mind.

"Hey," said Becky, standing up to answer the door, "I've got an idea. Let's ask Madelyn about the pageant and see what she thinks."

"Aw, c'mon, Becky, " I groaned. "She's so darn positive, I know she'll want me to go ahead with it."

Just as I'd anticipated, Madelyn was in full agreement with Becky.

"Why, Cheryl, honey," she said, her brow knit in earnest concern, "of course I think you should enter. God's blessed you with so many gifts, He wants you to use them. He wants you to win with them. The last thing he wants you to do is give up."

"Hoo-boy," I groaned. "I'm beginning to wish I'd never

mentioned this. I think you two had better run along now; Sammy and me, we've got a lesson to do—right, Sammy?"

As I patted the piano bench as a signal for Sammy to take his seat, the others—still talking about the Miss MSU pageant —left the room.

But for the remainder of the weekend, I couldn't stop thinking about what Becky and Madelyn had said; their words, like seeds of encouragement, had been firmly planted in my heart and were rapidly taking root. Not wanting to make any rash moves, I decided to mention the matter to Pam when I returned to school on Monday. Upon hearing her opinion, I'd then make my decision.

Pam's response, however, took me by surprise.

"Enter again?" she had cried, in a tone both incredulous and alarmed. "Oh, Cheryl, do you really think you should? What if you were to lose? I'd hate to see you get hurt again."

That did it. For another person to imply that I might not succeed made me want to compete for the title all the more. Thanks to Pam's unwitting use of reverse-psychology, once again I was in the running—albeit with less than my usual amount of enthusiasm and confidence.

It was more with a sense of plodding determination than starry-eyed enthusiasm that I began preparing for the pageant. Still, everything seemed to fall together with rather remarkable ease.

Once again, the brothers of Phi Gamma Delta were willing to sponsor me. My Talent routine, a stand-up performance of the bittersweet ballad "He Ain't Heavy . . . He's My Brother" was something I had always wanted to try. My clothes, too, were pretty much in order—from an earlier pageant, a bright peach swimsuit; for my Talent number, an unusual bronze one-shouldered dress; and for my evening gown, an elegant creation of lime-green Qiana, borrowed from—of all people—Patti Walton. My crooked front teeth had inadvertently been straightened months earlier, following a minor accident when I'd nearly lost them all. (On tour with the Madrigal Singers, I'd impulsively hopped on the shoulders of one of our brawnier baritones while boarding the homeward-bound bus. He, unfortunately, had been more startled than delighted by my gesture of affection; I fell off and landed flat on my face on the concrete pavement.) And to top it all off, there was a sale of quick-tanning lotion (a must for any serious swimsuit competitor) at the local drugstore.

The only thing not working toward my favor was—as usual—Daddy's ongoing refusal to support my involvement in pageants in any way.

One afternoon, a week or two prior to the pageant, I met Mother at Web Wood's drugstore in downtown Ackerman, where she had recently started working as a salesperson. (Due to increasingly poor business, we had had to close the store two years earlier. Having received her degree from Ole Miss, Paulette also worked at the drugstore as a pharmacist.)

"Mother," I said, as she walked behind the store's small soda fountain and began to pour me a Tab, "there are lots of folks who say I might win this pageant. It's my last chance to try, you know. Think there's any chance Daddy might come?"

"Doubt it," replied Mother, setting the small paper cup of cola in front of me. "You know Daddy." Picking up a damp cloth, she began to wipe the counter.

"Guess you're right," I said. "But I sure do wish he'd at least consider it. If he could only see what goes on at a pageant and what a good experience it is for the girls who participate—I really think he'd change his mind about the whole thing. You'll be there, won't you?"

"Sure will," said Mother. "Me, Paulette, Tim, Heath—the whole gang. We'll be rootin' for you, honey. Wouldn't miss it for the world."

"Great," I said, encouraged by Mother's enthusiasm.

Still, Daddy's lack of support was, for me, an underlying emotional drain. Whenever I thought about it too much, it was almost as though a part of me resisted from falling into synch with the total effort.

But as the big weekend approached, it was with unprecedented fervor and discipline that I proceeded full steam ahead toward my goal.

Night after night I sang my heart out in rehearsals with Becky. She, in turn, with a ruthless eye for style and detail, coached me in my Talent number like a pro. Having spent most of my performing life hidden behind a piano, my initial attempts as a stand-up singer were pathetically awkward. Funny, too.

"What's the matter with you?" laughed Becky, the first time I sang for her. "You look like a scared puppy—like you're afraid someone's going to take a poke at you. C'mon now, and loosen up! Extend those arms! Move those hips! Get down and boogie!"

Night after night, too, with the help of Paulette and Pam, I continued to be slathered with quick-tanning lotion. (If I were to apply it, my hands would turn orange.) It wasn't long before I looked as though I'd just returned from a ten-day cruise in the Bahamas.

"Better stick to sponge baths from here on out," joked Pam, the night before the pageant. "One good shower, and you'll come out looking like a zebra."

For all our hard work, I still wasn't prepared when, on the first night of judging at the Miss MSU pageant, the emcee called out my name as winner of the Swimsuit preliminary.

Earlier on, I'd already lost Talent, and my confidence—shaky from the start—was by this time at an all-time low. Certain that the emcee had made a mistake, I remained motionless in the line-up of thirty girls; better that, I reasoned, than to risk humiliating myself by having to return to my place once the emcee recognized his error and called out the true winner's name.

Suddenly, one of the girls next to me poked me in the ribs. "Psss-t!" she whispered, "Cheryl! Are you deaf? That's you! Get moving!"

With a shove more worthy of a football player than a pageant contestant, she pushed me forward.

Incredibly, it was true. I had won the Swimsuit preliminary. Point-wise, and in the eyes of the judges, it was an accomplishment as beneficial as winning Talent.

Even so, I was equally unprepared on the following and final night when I found myself among the ten finalists on center stage. One of us would be the new Miss MSU. One by one, runners-up were announced. I was still onstage.

Then it happened.

The emcee called my name.

I could hardly believe it.

I had won! I had done it! The new Miss MSU was none other than me—Cheryl Prewitt!

If only Daddy were here, I thought, as I stepped forward to receive my crown. *Then everything would be perfect.*

Five people suddenly entered my life as a result of winning the Miss MSU pageant—their primary purpose not only being to welcome and introduce me to my new role as campus representative—but also to prepare me for the upcoming Miss Mississippi pageant in Vicksburg.

Bill Foster, a slight, soft-spoken man, was MSU's Dean of Student Services. At this time of year, however, it became his and his wife Sara's self-appointed task to take me under their wing—not unlike a second daughter—for months of intensive training preceding the July pageant.

Likewise, Gail and Fred Rhodes, an attractive young couple in their early thirties, joined forces to lend me their help and expertise. Gail, MSU's Director of Student Affairs, was the person who was in charge of the Miss MSU pageant. Her husband, Fred, was a graduate student studying business administration.

The fifth person was William Stephens, a boyish and good-humored 1972 graduate of MSU. William worked as an admissions counselor for the school. At this time of year, however, he—like the others—spent countless hours coaching me in everything from makeup to wardrobe.

Though William had majored in English, his special interest was music; like myself, he had been singing and playing the piano since childhood. When, as Miss MSU, I began to receive numerous invitations to sing at campus and community functions, William often joined me as my accompanist.

Because of his years of experience, William was extremely helpful when it came to working on my Talent number. After hearing me sing "He Ain't Heavy . . . He's My Brother," he suggested that I try a more upbeat and showy song for the Miss Mississippi pageant. After much searching, we decided upon "Corner of the Sky," a jubilant number from the Broadway musical *Pippin*. Well-acquainted with many former Miss MSUs, William even went so far as to borrow from one of his friends my dress for the number—an extravagant silver gown with an ostrich feather plume.

The more we worked together, the more William intrigued me. Well into his twenties, he was the first real bachelor I'd ever known. Like the Fosters and the Rhodeses, he lived in Starkville. And though he shared an apartment with a roommate, sometimes he seemed lonely.

"William," I said one day, as we finished running through "Corner of the Sky" in the Fosters' living room, "tell me something. How did you ever get started in this kind of thing —you know, pageants and all?"

"Oh," he replied, "I don't know for sure. I guess it all started when I used to watch the Miss America pageant with my father and help him try to pick the winner. Then, when I was older, I had the opportunity to be an accompanist for a Miss Mississippi who later went on to win third runner-up to Phyllis George, who won Miss America that year. Boy, what I would have given to have been able to go to that pageant!

"Since then, I've really enjoyed helping Bill and Sara with our Miss MSUs. It's truly amazing what can happen with a little work. Why, we've seen girls literally be transformed from shy little caterpillar-types to gorgeous, confident butterflies!" William smiled. "You, however, are not one of those. You've already got what it takes—all the raw material, that is. All you need is a little refining."

"Refining?" I cried. "Thanks a lot! You make me sound like some backwoods hillbilly. I'm gettin' tired of your teasing."

"You're what?" asked William, with a playful grin.

"I'm gettin' tired of your teasing," I said.

"Gittin?" he mimicked.

"Gettin'," I snapped. "G-E-T-T-I-N-G."

"Oh-h," said William broadly, "*Getting*. Well, if that's what you mean, then you'd better learn how to say it."

The next day I was meeting with one of the school's speech professors for help with my diction. It was then, I think, that I realized for the first time the major difference between getting ready for local pageants and for the state competition in Vicksburg: this, for all its fun, was *serious*.

"Cheryl," Sara explained one evening as she watched me model one of her daughter's swimsuits, "I'm not sure you understand. Winning Miss Mississippi is just one step away from winning Miss America—and that's not just any pageant. Contenders for Miss America are tops—brilliant, talented, and, perhaps most importantly, articulate. After all, the woman who wins Miss America will spend a year representing this country at countless functions nationwide, from women's club luncheons to dinner at the White House. It's really quite

a job, and the judges are looking for a gal who's mature and
sharp enough to handle it."

"Oh," I said. "I never really thought about it that way. In
fact, I never really thought about it at all."

"Well," said Sara, her blue eyes twinkling, "you'd better.
Bill and I both think you very well could do it."

Sizing me up as I turned on my heels, Sara shook her head
and frowned. "Uh-uh," she said. "No good. Makes you look
too hippy. I think your best bet's the peach suit you wore at
Miss MSU."

"Fine," I said. Long ago I'd learned the benefits of trusting
others' judgments in areas that were their specialities. If there
was anyone who knew swimsuits, it was Sara Foster.

As the July pageant approached, I spent increasing
amounts of time with William, the Fosters, and the Rhodeses
—rehearsing my Talent routine, modeling clothes, drilling for
diction, and reviewing Mississippi history and current events
for upcoming interviews. Occasionally, when William and I
heard of another local pageant taking place, we'd travel as
spies to check out the competition. It was all very exciting,
and though I knew it wouldn't be easy, I, too, began to share
the others' growing conviction that I could win.

Other times, however, I felt confused—as though I might
not be ready for such an accomplishment. To win the title of
Miss Mississippi, and possibly Miss America, would mean that
I'd have to give up my senior year of college—not to mention
the remainder of my reign as Miss MSU. Besides, my family
would miss me, and the feeling would be mutual.

The week before the pageant I was home putting food
away from supper when Mother, her hands wrist-deep in
sudsy dishwater, spoke up.

"Talked to your Daddy, today," she said nonchalantly.
"He says he plans on going with us to Vicksburg, to see you
in your pageant."

Nearly dropping a dish of coleslaw on the floor, I yelped at the news. "You're kidding!" I cried. "Fan-tastic!"

"Best not to get all excited," said Mother, smiling. "He might hear you and then change his mind."

"Right," I agreed, but I found it hard not to dance with happiness.

Sponsored by the Vicksburg Jaycees, the Miss Mississippi pageant was a week-long affair, modeled exactly after the Miss America pageant. All activities took place within the huge two thousand–seat auditorium, and many were open to the public. Interviews, rehearsals, and preliminary judging took place throughout the early part of the week and by Saturday night—the final evening—the ten finalists (though they didn't know who they were) would already have been selected.

Also selected earlier in the week, in events open to the public, were the Swimsuit and Talent winners.

To my amazement, singing "Corner of the Sky," I won Talent.

Perhaps the biggest difference between the Miss Mississippi pageant and others I had been in was the fact that as contestants we were kept in near-isolation, housed in a local girls' school that was closed for the summer. In addition, we were each assigned a chaperone, or official Pageant Hostess (often the wife of a Vicksburg Jaycee), whose job it was to protect us from well-meaning but sometimes overbearing friends and relatives. The only time I was permitted to see William, the Rhodeses, the Fosters, or members of my family was for three-minute stage-door encounters on evenings following preliminary performances that were open to the public.

While in one sense the isolation was a lonely experience, it also gave me lots of time to think—and pray.

Everything had happened so fast. One minute I was an MSU co-ed majoring in music education and the next I was a contender for Miss America—or so others thought. And I did, too. It was just that so very much I hated the idea of giving up my senior year at MSU—even if it did mean being Miss America.

Such mixed feelings kept bouncing around in the back of my mind, never truly surfacing until the last night of the pageant.

Just as had taken place four months earlier at the Miss MSU pageant, there I was, standing among the ten finalists on center stage. And when the fourth through second runners-up had been announced, I was still in the running. One of us would be first runner-up. One of us would be the new Miss Mississippi.

Lord, I prayed silently in that moment, *I don't know if I want this. I don't know if I'm ready. Oh, Lord, if it's truly what You want for me, then go ahead. Let me win. Otherwise . . .*

Suddenly, to my indescribable relief and joy, I heard the emcee announce my name as first runner-up.

For once, it was easy to be a loser.

"Oh thank you," I cried, tears of happiness streaming down my face as I stepped forward to receive my trophy and scholarship award. "Thank you so very much!"

The scholarship award as first runner-up to Miss Mississippi was for $1,750. With that I'd be able to complete my senior year of college scot-free. No longer would I have to sell cosmetics to bring in extra money; and with the extra free time, I'd better be able to focus all my energies toward earning my degree. Moreover, I'd be able to fulfill my reign as Miss MSU.

The next morning, while heading home with the family, I sat in the front seat next to Daddy. For a long time, as the rest of us chattered like magpies about the preceding evening, he remained unusually quiet. Finally, some two hours into the one hundred fifty–mile drive, he spoke.

"Glad I came," he said gruffly.

"Oh, Daddy," I replied, squeezing his arm. "I'm glad you came, too!"

Wincing at my emotional response, he once again fell silent. Then, a few minutes later he spoke again.

"You coming back here again next year?" he asked.

The question took me by surprise. Thrilled at having come in as first runner-up, exhausted from the week's ordeal, the idea of returning to Vicksburg the following year—or ever—was about the furthest thing from my mind.

"Well," I replied, "I, uh, guess so."

"You guess so?" asked Daddy. "Well, I know so."

Miss State University. One of those many years I was a runner-up instead of the winner!

Gail Rhodes on the right, one of my judges and Pat Hopson on the left. Oh, by the way, pretty cute doll, huh?

During my Miss America year, I was with many state and local queens!

Competing for Miss Mississippi.

Finally being crowned Miss Mississippi.

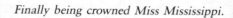

Friday night, Miss America pageant, I won the preliminary swimsuit competition, Tana Kay Carley won the preliminary talent competition.

There she is, Miss Mississippi!

*Briggs and Pat Hopson —
don't know if I could have
done it without them!*

USO was not very glamorous!

During my year as Miss America I went on a USO (United Service Organization) tour with my troupe to Asia!

Do you choose to be happy today?

You decide how it's gonna be! It's up to you!

SPEEDING EASTWARD on Mississippi State Highway 12, the winter landscape looked especially bleak. Even the cattle seemed to regard me with lonely stares.

It was January 1979 and I was returning to school for my final semester as a senior. It had been a great year so far; as Miss MSU, I'd made over two hundred appearances (my favorites were singing "The Star-Spangled Banner" at ball games) and many new friends. Still, my mood was as gray as the cold afternoon sky as I pulled into the dormitory parking lot and began unloading my car.

To the casual observer it would seem that my room had everything I needed—posters, popcorn popper, Crock-Pot, fridge. There was one thing, however, I didn't have—and that was Pam.

Engaged to be married in the spring to Greg Roberts (an MSU student who had graduated the year before), Pam had attended summer school which had enabled her to graduate in December. Though I knew my new roommate would be nice enough, I also knew that I'd miss Pam terribly. Recalling our last days together, I felt a lump in my throat.

It had been in December, just before the Christmas break. For weeks the two of us—not wanting to face up to the fact of our imminent separation—had been avoiding our evening prayer time together. Both of us feared that the moment we sat down and actually started talking about the subject, we'd probably start crying.

Sure enough, we did.

"Oh, Cheryl," Pam had sobbed, "it's so hard to say goodbye. I'm gonna miss you so much—more than you'll ever know."

"I know," I'd agreed. "You're one of the best friends I ever had."

Later, after finally composing ourselves, we prayed, thanking the Lord for our friendship and for all the wonderful times we had shared. Then, over steaming mugs of cocoa and far into the night, we talked.

"You know," Pam had said, "it's funny how people most always get what they really want out of life, in the end. Take me, for instance; all my life, I've wanted to marry, settle down, and raise a family. Even so, now that it's about to happen, I can hardly believe it's true!"

"I know what you mean," I'd replied. "Greg's such a great guy, too. I know you're both gonna be so happy. And I can't wait to be in your wedding!"

Pam, however, seemed not to hear me.

"Cheryl," she said thoughtfully, "what is it that you want out of life? That's something I've never heard you talk about. Is it marriage? Or a career?"

"Why not both?" I'd laughed—and then quickly changed the subject. Pam's question had struck a sensitive nerve.

What did I want?

It was a question I'd asked myself a lot in recent months, yet never seemed to have found the answer. Most kids seemed to know exactly what they wanted at this stage of their college career; everyone I knew was either engaged to be married, lining up job interviews, or applying for graduate school. For some strange reason, none of these choices applied—or appealed—to me.

While graduate school remained a possibility, I was anxious to be out of a university environment, in the world, and putting to use what I'd learned.

And as far as marriage was concerned, I knew I wasn't ready. To begin with, I didn't even have a steady; in fact, I had never had one. Whenever I felt myself getting serious over someone, I had the darndest habit of breaking it off. For fear of getting tied down, I never allowed myself to get too close to anyone. I felt, somehow, that commitment to another might prevent me from reaching my dreams.

But what dreams?

In four months I'd be graduating with my long-awaited degree in music education—but for what? Often I recalled Becky's words when she had encouraged me to enter my first pageant: "There's a great big world waiting for you out there," she had said. "I just see so much more for you than a future spent teaching piano to kids and singing gospel music on the weekends."

More importantly, I remembered the vivid calling I had felt for missionary work in my freshman year. Often I found myself bursting with desire to witness about the power and love of God on a grand scale. Though I kept my eyes open for opportunities in this area, none ever seemed to arise.

"Lord," I had finally prayed over the Christmas holidays at home, "show me what it is You want me to do with my life. Open the doors that will let me serve You the best I can. Give me the opportunity, and I promise I'll take hold of it and give it all I've got."

Now, as I unloaded the car, my eyes glimpsed a poster that had become wedged beneath the spare tire in my trunk. On it was a smiling picture of myself as Miss MSU, encouraging students to attend our basketball games. I smiled ironically. It was the same poster that only one year earlier had inspired me to try for the title of Miss MSU. Scenes of those happy days flashed through my mind . . . Becky and Madelyn's initial encouragement . . . meeting William, the Rhodeses, and the Fosters . . . coming in as first runner-up in the Miss Mississippi pageant . . . and Daddy's curious statement on the day we had driven home.

Isn't it odd, I mused, *how certain Daddy was that I would return to Vicksburg to compete again for the title of Miss Mississippi?* I slammed the trunk shut and headed for the dorm. *What good could possibly come from doing such a thing?*

Of course, it would be an altogether different story if I did win and went on to win Miss America, too. What a turn my life would take then! Winning the title of Miss America would be much like landing a job—a fabulous job that would take me traveling not only across America, but around the world, too. Just think of the witnessing I could do. Why, it was just the job I'd been dreaming of . . .

Suddenly, I stopped in my tracks, struck with the realization that my involvement in pageants could, in fact, be a means to an end—that is, if my ultimate goal was to win the title of Miss America!

Could this, I wondered, *be the answer I'd been praying for? Could trying for the title of Miss America be what God wanted me to do with my life; that is, if my purpose was to use the position as a means of witnessing for Him on a world-wide scale?* The more I thought and prayed about it, the more certain I became that it was.

The following weekend when I mentioned the matter to Daddy, he agreed wholeheartedly.

"You do what you have to do," he said. "Your mother and I will support you all the way."

A few days later, I phoned William to tell him my plans. While he didn't seem as enthused as I had hoped, he agreed to meet me in the piano room of my dorm (a small room off the main lobby) to talk about the subject further.

"Well," William responded thoughtfully, after hearing me speak, "I don't see what's to keep you from trying. But it sure beats me where you get your confidence. You seem so sure of yourself—about what you want to do with your life."

"It's not so much what I want to do," I replied, "but what God wants me to do."

"What?" said William. "How can you say that?"

"I've been praying about it," I said. "And I've come to believe that this is my year to win Miss America. It's just a feeling—a certainty—deep down in my spirit. That's about the only way I can describe it."

"I sure wish I could feel that way," said William. "I get so low sometimes—so unsure about the future."

"You believe in Jesus, don't you?" I asked.

"I guess so," he replied. "That is, I was raised in the Church."

"Well, then," I said, "you know as well as anyone that God loves you and has a wonderful plan for your life. All you have to do is ask Him to reveal it to you. You know—ask, seek, knock. Is there a church you go to now?"

"Uh-uh," William shook his head. "Don't know why, really. Guess I never got around to finding one. Besides, Sunday morning is my only day to sleep in."

"Why don't you try going with the Fosters sometime?" I suggested. "They seem to belong to a real lively congregation. In fact, I recently heard from Sara that they're growing so fast, they're meeting at a local restaurant until they can build a new building. It's okay to be a Christian all by yourself," I smiled, "but it's so much more fun being part of a family of believers! It's so good for your spirit. Besides, in church—if it's a good one—you not only enjoy fellowship, but also get good Bible teaching and a regular chance to worship."

"What you say is very likely true," replied William, "and maybe I'll try it sometime. But the state of my spiritual life isn't the reason we called this meeting, is it?" He grinned. "If you are so dead set on winning Miss America, my dear, we've got a lot of work to do."

William was right.

For starters, I had to find a local pageant to enter—and win —that would enable me to compete once again for the title of Miss Mississippi in Vicksburg. (I could not enter a second time as Miss MSU.) After some searching, I decided to enter the Miss Starkville pageant, a relatively small local event, usually overshadowed by the Miss MSU competition.

While I didn't like the idea, I knew it would be necessary

to keep my participation in the Miss Starkville pageant quiet until the last possible minute; word of my entering might cause younger, less experienced girls to drop out. Unfortunately, some two weeks before the pageant, that's exactly what began to happen and I found myself practically begging friends to enter in order to maintain the pageant's required five-contestant minimum. Thanks to pretty, dark-haired Terri Smith, a friend from my floor who agreed to enter, the show went on.

The day before the pageant, which took place in mid-May, I had everything I needed but a new Talent routine. While I knew I could always fall back on "He Ain't Heavy . . . He's My Brother" or "Corner of the Sky," I didn't think that repeating a past performance would reflect too well on me in the eyes of the judges.

Now in a near-panic state, I was at William's apartment, listening to tapes of several popular songs, desperately hoping that we might discover something suitable. With one more tape to go, I'd more or less decided upon "Can You Read My Mind," the dreamy theme from the movie *Superman*. Pretty though the tune was, it didn't seem to go anywhere.

"Wait a minute," William said. "Before we decide, just listen to this last tape. It's a new song sung by Melissa Manchester, called 'Don't Cry Out Loud.' Listen to the lyrics. I think you'll like them."

Sighing, I agreed. Already I didn't like the song's title; too negative. But then I heard the words:

Baby cried the day the circus came to town,
  'Cause she didn't like parades just passing by her.
So she painted on a smile and took up with some clown,
  And she danced without a net upon the wire.
I know a lot about her 'cause you see—
  Baby is an awful lot like me.

And then, the chorus:

Don't cry out loud.
Just keep it inside.
Learn how to hide your feelings.
Fly high and proud.
And if you should fall,
    Remember you almost had it all!

"Wow!" I exclaimed, when the tape had finished. "I really like it! I'm not so crazy about the idea of hiding your feelings, but the part about trying and not giving up—I really like it. Besides, the melody's powerful, and the range is good, too."

"I thought you'd go for it," grinned William. "Let's get busy rehearsing."

Still in the process of memorizing the words to "Don't Cry Out Loud," I entered the Miss Starkville pageant—and won. Terri Smith came in as first runner-up.

The one unusual moment during the Miss Starkville pageant occurred when, just as the winner was about to be announced, I heard myself whispering the following prayer:

"Lord," I had said, "this is Your pageant. If I can do more good for You—reach more people—as Miss Starkville than as plain old me, then let me win. Otherwise, don't."

Never had I prayed like that before any pageant; but for some reason I sensed that to do so was somehow necessary— that it was what God expected from me if I wanted to make it to Atlantic City knowing for sure that I was in His will.

From the moment I won the title of Miss Starkville, between preparing for final exams and my senior piano recital, every waking hour was spent getting ready for the upcoming Miss Mississippi pageant.

This was it, I realized. Do or die.

Also preparing for the Miss Mississippi pageant was the newly crowned Miss MSU. For this reason, the Fosters and the Rhodeses—while excited about my plans to enter again—

were understandably unable to spend as much time with me as they had in the past. William and I, however, continued to see a lot of each other.

One day in late May, the two of us were in the piano room, running through a mock interview in preparation for Vicksburg. With William as my interrogator, the session had proceeded fairly well; after four years of pageants, I was an old hand at fielding questions on everything from women's rights to famous moments in Mississippi history. I thought we had finished when William, in his most officious judge's voice said, "Tell me, Miss Prewitt, for what reason, may I ask, have you chosen to enter this pageant? Your information sheet tells me that you already competed for the title of Miss Mississippi last year. Why go through it again?"

"Well sir," I replied, "I've entered this pageant for one reason and one reason only—and that's to win."

"Cheryl!" exclaimed William, suddenly falling out of character. "How can you talk like that? What's more, *why* do you talk like that? What if you lose? You'll look like a fool."

"I'm not going to lose," I said. "I'm going to win. And the reason I talk like this is because there's power in confessing what you know in your spirit to be true."

"What?" he asked. "What do you mean, 'power in confessing'? I thought confessing had something to do with sin."

"No, no," I said, laughing. "This kind of confessing I'm talking about is more like positive thinking — I guess you could call it positive talking. There's power in it. Consider what Jesus said in Mark 11:23 RSV, 'Truly, I *say* to you, whoever *says* to this mountain, "Be taken up and cast into the sea," and does not doubt in his heart, but believes what he *says* will come to pass, it will be done for him.' You see, William, not only do you have to believe, you've got to *say* what you believe. Confess it to others.

"Your mind can be so stubborn when it comes to accepting spiritual truths," I continued. "The way I figure it, confessing with your mouth helps your mind to become convinced. It also serves to surround you with continual positive vibrations—like a protective screen—that prevent Satan from sabotaging your mind with negativity. You know, things like doubt and fear. Satan, see, hates anything positive because he knows he can't beat it. He's absolutely helpless to penetrate healthy, positive attitudes."

"There you go again," said William, rolling his eyes in exasperation, "so doggone sure about everything. What do you plan to tell the judges when they ask you where you get your confidence?"

"Same thing I just told you," I said. "What else? Unless God changes my heart, I'm positive it's His will that I go on to become Miss Mississippi and then Miss America."

"I don't know," said William, shaking his head. "It's too deep for me."

By midsummer, I was pretty well fixed for the Vicksburg competition. From Kathy Foster (Sara and Bill's sixteen-year-old daughter) I'd borrowed a pretty powder-blue swimsuit, and with the help of Mother and a seamstress friend, I'd been able to fashion a striking ruby-red sequined, slit-to-the-knee Talent dress. In the eyes of pageant judges every detail counts, and though I sometimes worried about the shoes that went with my Talent dress—a pair of red, high-heeled mules (backless sandals with thick wooden soles that I had also borrowed from Kathy)—they were the best we could do.

What really had me concerned was finding a suitable evening gown. Though we'd looked and looked, we couldn't seem to find what we wanted anywhere. Moreover, I didn't have much money to spend.

Finally, as a last resort, we decided to pool our talents as designers/dressmakers. In one mad, thirty-minute shopping spree in downtown Columbus' largest fabric store, five of us

—Sara, Kathy, William, Paulette, and myself—scooped up pattern, fabric, half-price lace, approximately thirty-five packages of assorted sequins and bugle beads, and two large bottles of Elmer's Glue-All. Total cost: $45.00.

Once the basic dress had been made (a simple, off-white, spaghetti-strap gown), the rest of our time was spent covering the creation with thousands of tiny sequins and beads. For two solid days and nights we worked on the project, spreading the dress—like a blanket of sparkling confection— across Bill and Sara's dining-room table.

Late in the second day, the five of us were knuckle-deep in glue and bugle beads when Bill Foster suddenly entered through the back door—huffing and puffing from his nightly jog around the neighborhood.

"How y'all doing?" he asked, flopping into a nearby easy chair.

"Great," replied Sara. "We've been waiting for you. Pull up a chair and start gluing."

"In a minute," grinned Bill, raising his hand as if to protest. "Gotta catch my breath first." Still, he kept on talking. "I was jogging tonight with Dr. Rose," he went on, "chairman of our board of deacons. We're holding the dedication service for our new church tomorrow, and when he heard Cheryl was in town, he wondered if she might do us a favor and sing as part of the program.

"Cheryl," he raised his eyebrows, "think you might be able to do that?"

"Sure," I agreed. "If William, here, would be willing to accompany me." I looked over at William, who was seated across the table. "Would you do that for me?" I asked.

"Why not?" he grinned, holding up ten sparkling fingertips. "Anything's better than this."

Later, I wondered what it was that had prompted me to ask William for assistance, when I could have just as easily accompanied myself. For some strange reason, however, it had seemed the right thing to do.

The following morning we met for the dedication service in the back room of Starkville's Bonanza Steakhouse, where members of the Faith Baptist Church were meeting until their new building was completed. The L-shaped private dining room afforded twice the space of their old structure; even so, by the time the service started, the room was full.

When it was time for me to perform for the congregation, I sang one of my favorite contemporary gospel songs, "Give Them All to Jesus." The song speaks of surrendering all—your cares, troubles, worries, and fears—to Jesus, trusting that He knows your every need and wants to take care of you. Once while singing I glanced at William and was surprised to see him uncharacteristically misty-eyed with emotion. Later in the service, when the pastor extended an invitation for members to reaffirm their faith and for visitors to become charter members of the new church, I was even more surprised to see William leave his piano bench and join those who had accepted the invitation. Wide-eyed, I watched as he walked to the front of the room, talked for some time with the preacher, bowed his head in prayer, and returned to his seat glowing like a neon light.

When the service ended, I joined the others who were rearranging chairs and tables for the Sunday dinner that was to follow. Suddenly, I felt someone come up from behind and hug me. It was William.

"Cheryl," he beamed, "I can't thank you enough for what happened this morning."

"What do you mean?" I asked.

"I reaffirmed my faith," he said. "I joined the church! It's so strange—I mean, from the moment I arrived here I was overwhelmed with a sense that this is where I belonged. Where I was supposed to be. Like you said some time ago, I realized how much I needed the fellowship, the teaching, the worship that only a church can offer. And you know what? The preacher mentioned that there's an opening for a new music director and I might very well fit the bill!"

"Oh, William," I cried, "that's wonderful news! I thought something was going on in your spirit when I caught you looking so misty-eyed during our song."

"It was the song that cinched it," said William. "That is, the lyrics. For the first time I grasped what you've been telling me for so long—how much God loves us and how He really does have a plan for our lives—if we'll only ask Him to reveal it. I've been a believer for most my life, but it took me until today to realize those simple truths.

"I'm even," he continued, with a twinkle in his eye, "beginning to believe all that talk of yours about confessing victories before they happen. That's not to say, however, that I'm about to put down cold cash for a ticket to Atlantic City."

"Would you consider making a reservation?" I asked with mock-seriousness.

"You got it," he grinned.

In Vicksburg, on the morning of the final day of the Miss Mississippi pageant, my spirit may have been confident, but my mind was beginning to wonder. Even though I'd won Talent the night before, I was definitely suffering a mild case of butterflies as I applied my makeup and prepared to face the grueling day and evening ahead. Should I find myself named as a finalist—and chances were good that I would—the judging process would begin again. One more time I'd be called to walk in my swimsuit. One more time I'd be called to perform my Talent routine.

It had been an exhausting week. Moreover, I was lonely. While last year I hadn't minded the isolation of the competition, this year it bothered me. Though my tiny room was crowded with cards and flowers from Pam, Becky, my family, and others, they were no substitute for the real thing.

Suddenly, my thoughts were interrupted by a knock at the door. It was my chaperone. In her hand, she held a brown paper bag.

"Cheryl," she said, "there was a lady downstairs asking for you. Sara was her name. She knew she couldn't see you, but she wanted me to give you this."

"Thanks," I said, taking the bag. "Appreciate it."

I returned to my vanity and sat down. While opening the bag, which I assumed contained some health-food snack such as cheese or apples, a note fell out and fluttered to the floor. Reaching down to pick it up, I recognized Sara's handwriting.

"Wear these tonight for Talent," the hastily scrawled message read. "And don't ask any questions."

Puzzled, I reached into the bag and cried out in dismay as I pulled out two of the ugliest red shoes I had ever seen.

High-heeled sandals, the shoes (which looked as though they must have originally been beige) had been painted crimson and dipped in red glitter. Still sticky to the touch, they reminded me of some sort of failed arts-and-crafts project. At the bottom of the bag were cottonballs and a small bottle of paint thinner.

What is this? I thought. *Some kind of a joke?*

While Kathy's red mules might not have been the greatest shoes, these were hideous.

But Sara, I knew, was not the type who played jokes; her desire for me to do the best I could at tonight's competition was as strong as my own. Besides, when it came to clothes, Sara's judgment was impeccable. There must, therefore, be some valid reason for her wanting me to wear these horrible shoes.

Sighing, I removed Kathy's wood-soled mules from the top

shelf of the closet and replaced them with Sara's creation. And as I did, I almost had to laugh. The shoes, for all their tackiness, reminded me of something from the Land of Oz— hand-me-downs, perhaps, from the wardrobe of Glinda, the Good Witch of the North.

That night, honoring Sara's request, I wore the red shoes for my Talent number. Though with every step I felt them sticking to the bottom of my feet, they must not have hurt my performance too badly; judges and audience alike responded to "Don't Cry Out Loud" with thunderous applause that lasted a full five minutes.

A short while later, I found myself in the same position I'd been in the year before—a top ten finalist listening with all my might for the emcee's next words. Runners-up four through one had already been announced. One of us would be the next Miss Mississippi.

This time, however, I had no second thoughts. I had no mixed feelings. This time, I wanted to win.

Silently, I prayed my pageant prayer.

Lord, this is Your pageant. If I can do more good for You —reach more people—as Miss Mississippi than as Miss Stark-ville, then let me win. Otherwise, don't.

With that, I heard the emcee announce my name.

I'd done it! I'd won!

The moments immediately following were an exciting blur of congratulations, roses, tears, and happiness like I'd never known. After the pageant, officials whisked me away and escorted me to the Queen's Ball, a late-night gala held at the Vicksburg Country Club. There, at last, I had plenty of time to visit with friends and family. Everyone, it seemed, was there—Mother and Daddy, Madelyn, Becky, Paulette, William, and—of course—Bill and Sara.

"Glad to see you wore your shoes," grinned Sara, glancing down at my ankles which were streaked with bright red paint from the shoes' still-wet straps. (In the excitement of winning, I hadn't yet had a chance to apply the paint thinner.)

"Oh, Sara!" I cried, "thanks for sending them to me. I've got to admit, though, you sure had me worried when they first arrived. I thought you were playing a joke."

Sara laughed.

"They were pretty funny-looking, weren't they?" she said. "But oh, Cheryl, from a distance, onstage, they were *gorgeous*—so sparkly and dainty—much better than those old mules of Kathy's. William and I knew something had to be done after watching you perform last night.

"Early this morning we searched every shoe store in Vicksburg until we finally found ourselves at one of those huge discount places—you know, where all the shoes are displayed on racks? Well, after picking out the cheapest pair of high-heeled sandals we could find, we rushed 'em back to the Holiday Inn, dumped 'em in the tub with newspapers and spray-painted 'em red, doused 'em with glitter, dried 'em best we could on top of the air-conditioning unit, and rushed 'em on over to you as fast as possible."

"Any chance you prayed over them?" I grinned.

"Nope," said Sara, shaking her head. "That's about the only thing we didn't do."

"Well, someone must have," I winked. "'Cause if you ask me, those old shoes were blessed."

IT WAS JUST PAST NOON the afternoon after the pageant, but already it had been a long day.

Following three hour's sleep after the Queen's Ball, I'd awakened to pack, dress, and head for the Miss Mississippi Awards Brunch, where rewards and recognition continued. Highlight of the brunch was when I was presented with the keys to a brand new car—my very own Chrysler Le Baron. (Good-bye, Green Machine!)

Now, seated in the driver's seat, I was joined by Pat Hopson, an Associate Hostess of the Miss Mississippi pageant. Together, we were about to depart for Pat's home in suburban Vicksburg, where several Miss Mississippi pageant committee board members were waiting for me to sign my contract and to answer any questions I or any members of my family might have. Mother, Daddy, and Heath would follow in a car behind us. Paulette and Tim had already returned home.

Pat, a soft-spoken woman with smiling eyes, was married to Dr. Briggs Hopson, a prominent Vicksburg surgeon. Earlier in the week, when I'd first met the Hopsons, I'd been struck by their warmth and gracious manner. The two made a charming couple; Briggs, with his casual, intellectual Ivy League look, and Pat, with her bell-like laugh and graceful carriage. Moreover, both shared a down-home sense of humor and loving nature that reminded me much of Sara and Bill Foster.

Pat was the woman who would be accompanying me as my official chaperone to Atlantic City. And, with the Miss America pageant only six short weeks away, I would be staying as a guest at the Hopson's home until our time of departure.

As I turned on the ignition of my new car and began to back out of the parking lot, I noticed Pat carefully buckling her seat belt. There was something about the act—something too deliberate and more than careful—that caused me to catch my breath. As Pat turned to face me, the bright midday sun picked out a pattern of thin, pink scars that crisscrossed the right side of her face. I'd never noticed them before.

"You've been in a car wreck, haven't you?" I asked.

"Why yes," Pat replied. "How did you know?"

"The way you fastened your seat belt," I said. "Forgive me for being so blunt, but I was in a wreck once, too. Not much fun, are they?"

Pat shook her head, a vague shadow of fear crossing her face at the memory of the incident.

"Tell me about it," I said. "What happened?"

"It was nine months ago," said Pat. "Halloween night. Briggs and I were on the interstate, heading home from a play, when we ran into a car that had stopped in our lane with no lights on. I wasn't wearing my seat belt. First my head hit the dash, taking off the right side of my face. Then I hit the windshield. The impact was so hard, it left a molded impression of my face in the shattered glass. Doctors worked on my face for four hours that night at the hospital—I don't know how many stitches they took—but there's still a lot of work that remains to be done. It's much improved, though."

"Gosh," I said, "it sounds like you're lucky to have lived."

"Lucky isn't the word," said Pat. "It's a miracle. Minutes before the accident I happened to fall asleep, and experts say that's what saved my life. My slumped, relaxed position prevented me from being thrown completely through the windshield and likely winding up decapitated."

"No!" I cried.

"It's true," said Pat. "The Lord was looking out for me that night, and that's all there is to it. Tell me, what happened to you?"

"Well," I said, "like you, I really feel the Lord was looking out for me, too."

And as I began to tell Pat my story—about my accident

and doctors saying I'd never walk again, and about my short leg being lengthened through prayer—I became aware that through our shared experiences and similar attitude toward God, a bond had been formed between the two of us that was very special.

"Can you see my scars?" I asked, as I finished my story. "Here—on my forehead, chin, and upper lip."

"Why, yes," said Pat, surprised. "I can. Funny, I never noticed them before."

"I can see your scars, too," I said. "But you want to know something I learned a long time ago? Our scars are visible to us, only because we know. Other people don't even notice them."

"Well, that's encouraging," said Pat. "I'm so glad we've had this talk. I feel as though I know you so well."

"I feel the same way," I said.

When we arrived at Pat's home, I was at first taken aback by its splendor. Never had I seen such a beautiful dwelling; a magnificent colonial-style building, it looked as though it were right out of Williamsburg. Filled with antiques and oriental rugs, its century-old hardwood floors had been shipped in by a friend from Underground Atlanta, and the bricks in the foyer had been taken from the original cobblestone streets of antebellum Vicksburg. Just beyond the entrance-way was a sunlit garden room with an eighteen-foot ceiling and bank of windows nearly as high. French doors opened out to a patio courtyard and lushly wooded backyard.

Still, for all my elegant surroundings, I felt right at home at the Hopsons'—especially after meeting their children; sixteen-year-old Kathy, eleven-year-old Jay, and fourteen-year-old Briggs Hopson III—better known as Bubba. Twenty-year-old Karen was away at college.

Dropping off my bags in the guest room, I returned downstairs where everyone, including Mother and Daddy, was waiting for me to sign my contract as "Miss Mississippi,

1980"—a one-year agreement which included bookings for several statewide appearances, more than $1,000 in gift certificates from local stores (most of which would be spent in preparing my wardrobe for the Miss America Pageant), and—should I choose to continue my education at some future time—a $2,000 scholarship.

For a fleeting moment, my heart skipped a beat as I signed my name to the document. *Everything is happening so fast. Am I signing my life away?* But from start to finish, the Hopsons (and many of the pageant board members) had been by our side, answering legal questions, reassuring Mother and Daddy that I would be well taken care of, and generally serving to make all of us feel comfortable.

Before I knew it, it was time for my family to leave.

"Good-bye, Mother," I said. "Good-bye, Daddy." I turned to Heath. "Now you take good care of these two for me, hear?"

Heath nodded earnestly.

Suddenly, noting Mother's teary eyes, I hugged her tightly.

"Now don't you worry about me," I said. "I'm gonna be just fine!"

Biting her lower lip, Mother nodded.

"So long, sweetheart," said Daddy, enveloping me with a big bear hug. "We'll be seeing you again before you leave for Atlantic City, won't we?"

Not knowing what to say, I looked to the Hopsons.

"Hard to tell," said Briggs. "From past experience, I'd say your daughter's going to be pretty busy from here on out."

"Well then," said Daddy, "I guess this is good-bye. Take care now, Cheryl. We'll be praying for you." He turned to Mother. "Right, Carrie Lou?"

Mother nodded.

"Thanks, Daddy," I said. "Thanks, Mother. Oh, thank you all so much for everything. I'm sure gonna miss you!"

With that, they were gone.

Still too excited from the past few day's events to succumb to tears, I flopped down on the garden-room love seat. Just as I was about to close my eyes, the telephone rang.

"I'll get it," said Pat. "You stay put."

Moments later, she returned.

"Well," she said, "looks as though we're off and running. That was Ada Duckett, your wardrobe designer. Ada's the woman who will be making all your Miss America gowns. She says we'll have to hustle if we want to get you outfitted in time. She'll be here in twenty minutes for your fitting, then she's off to Texas."

"Why Texas?" I asked. "To meet with another pageant contestant?"

"Oh, no," laughed Pat. "Ada's yours, and yours alone. She's one of the country's best designers. She lives in Texas."

"Oh," I said, trying not to sound too surprised. "That's really something."

"You'll love her," said Pat. "Her gowns are fabulous."

Two hours later, Ada had come and gone, and I was upstairs slipping back into my jeans and T-shirt. True to Pat's words, Ada's gowns promised to be fabulous. For Talent, she had suggested an ultrasophisticated black lace sheath that shimmered with thousands of tiny red, gold, and silver rhinestones. "To sparkle in the spotlight," Ada had said. For my evening gown, she envisioned a full-skirted floral creation in hues of blue, pink, and lavender, with one shoulder bare and the other hugged by four slender straps of sparkling rhinestones. "To match your crown," Ada had winked.

Suddenly, I heard a rap on the door.

"Sorry to rush you," said Pat, poking her head in the doorway. "But we've got to get all your pageant information to Atlantic City as soon as possible. This happens to us every year; the Miss Mississippi pageant is the last to take place and for that reason we always have to push a little harder than the others. First thing we're going to have to do is decide what your Talent number's going to be."

"My Talent number?" I asked. "Won't I be doing the same performance I did last night?"

"Most likely," Pat replied. "But maybe not. When you're ready, come on downstairs and we'll talk about it."

Not bothering to put on shoes, I ran downstairs to join Briggs, Pat, and several pageant board members who were waiting for me in the garden room.

"Have a seat," grinned Briggs, gesturing to the piano that was nestled beneath the stairway leading up to the second floor balcony. "We like your performance of 'Don't Cry Out Loud,' but why don't we hear a few others before deciding for sure? Besides, we'd love to hear you play. Pat mentioned that you once performed for the Jackson Symphony."

"My pleasure," I smiled and sat down at the piano to sing and play a variety of popular songs including "Corner of the Sky," "Tomorrow," and "Main Event."

"Wow!" Briggs exclaimed, when I had finished. "That's great! I'd only heard you sing before—I never knew you could play so well, too. You know, this gives me an idea: I think we should stick to 'Don't Cry Out Loud' for your song, but would you object to both singing *and* playing for the Miss America Pageant? You're so good at both, it's a shame to let either talent go unused."

"Object?" I said. "Not at all! Piano's always been my first love anyway."

"Good," said Briggs, making a notation on an official-looking form. "What do you think about starting the number seated at the piano, then leaving the bench for a knock-'em-dead, stand-up finish?"

"Sounds great," I said, and I began to work on the new routine that very afternoon.

The following evening I joined Briggs in his book-lined study to go over my Miss America contestant fact sheet, a page of information which would be considered not only by the judges, but would also be released to the press. The fact sheet, according to Pat, was Briggs's speciality. With his sharp eye for detail and keen sense of what the judges would be looking for, he took special care to tailor it to my best advantage.

"Hm-m," he said, adjusting his glasses as he studied the sheet. "I see here you've listed cooking as one of your hobbies. Tell me, how do you make a crepe?"

"A crepe?" I said. "Gosh, I don't know."

"Well then," said Briggs, "how do you make a soufflé?"

"Soufflé?" I repeated. "I'm afraid I don't know that, either."

"Well," said Briggs, regarding me curiously, "what kind of foods can you cook?"

"Oh," I said, "you know—things like black-eyed peas, country-fried chicken, homemade corn bread—"

"Ah-h," grinned Briggs, "you mean *southern* cooking."

"That's right," I said, watching as he carefully penned the word "southern" in on the fact sheet. "I guess I never thought of it that way before."

"It's a little thing," said Briggs. "But it makes a lot of difference. What if the judges were to ask you the same questions I did?"

"I see what you mean," I said, suddenly grateful to this new friend—only yesterday a near stranger—who now, on his own time and for no reward, was expressing such generous care and concern for me.

Suddenly, Pat poked her head in the doorway.

"You two still working on the fact sheet?" she asked.

"Um-hm," answered Briggs. "We're almost done. All that's left are a few lines for 'Interesting Facts.' Have any ideas?"

"Well," I said, "we could mention my sister and brothers

and the fact that we've been performing as a gospel group for so many years."

"That's good," said Briggs.

For a moment the room was silent, save for the scratch of his pen on the paper. Then Pat spoke up.

"I think you should mention your accident," she said.

"My accident?" I responded. "Why?"

"Well," said Pat, "it seems to me that your accident—and the events that resulted from it—make up the most important episodes of your life. In a very real way, it served to shape you into the person you are today. It's too important to leave out."

"But what if the judges and the press ask me questions about it?" I asked.

"I think you can trust the Lord will help you," said Pat. "And if it's something He wants to use to lead others to Him, you can be darn sure He will."

So, at the very bottom of the page, on the last line under "Interesting Facts," we wrote: "When I was 11 years old, I was in a terrible car wreck. Doctors said I'd never walk again, but through faith in God, I did."

That's all we wrote. No more, no less. But should anyone ask me about the incident, I was prepared to tell them all I knew.

Later that evening, when I was alone with Pat, we continued making plans for my six-week training program.

"There's lots to do," Pat said. "You've got what it takes to win, but you definitely need some polishing—refining, you might say."

I winced, recalling William's similar remark a year earlier.

"The first thing to tend to," continued Pat, "is your accent. You've got a stubborn twang—more country than southern—that's got to go. You'll also have to bone up for your interviews; at the national level, they can be pretty tough. Briggs and I subscribe to most all the newsmagazines;

during the day, it would be a good idea if you read and studied them for current events. I've also got some typed fact sheets about Mississippi, U.S. history, and the national government that you'll want to memorize. Later this week, we'll conduct your first mock interview. What we'll do is videotape the sessions, and then play them back for review. It's a great method—especially for cultivating a good on-screen presence."

"Videotape?" I said. "Wow, that's new to me."

The following Friday, the day of my first videotaped mock interview, found me nervous as a cat. Though I had drilled myself mercilessly in preparation for the event, for some reason the prospect of being interviewed on camera terrified me.

It was all to be very professional—just the way it would be in Atlantic City. My "interviewers" (pageant board members) would question me in the family room, where the camera was set up. A "monitor" would introduce me and call "time," when the seven minute time limit had passed. Until it was time for me to be introduced, I stayed hidden in the kitchen.

"I don't know why I'm so scared," I said to Pat, as she dabbed my nose with powder before leaving me to join the others.

"Now don't you worry about a thing," she said reassuringly. "This first interview will be very easy. Just remember to try not to close your eyes while you answer questions. I know you're simply trying to think on your feet, but it looks as though you've gone to sleep! Remember, too, to watch your accent and try not to answer every question with the preface 'basically.' I don't know where you picked up that habit. And above all, don't forget to smile!"

"Got it," I said.

Though my voice was confident, my heart was racing with fright as I glanced for one last time at the neatly typed list of

"Famous Mississippians" (topic for this evening's interview)
that I held in my trembling hands:

FAMOUS ROCK AND ROLL SINGER: Elvis Presley.

FAMOUS OPERA SINGER: Leontyne Price.

FAMOUS NOVELIST: William Faulkner.

FAMOUS SHORT-STORY WRITER: Eudora Welty . . .

With names and occupations swirling in my head, I joined
the others in the family room, where my five interrogators
were seated on an L-shaped sofa, waiting for me. Behind
them was the camera which was aimed, gunlike, straight toward the empty ice cream–parlor chair where I would be sitting.

"Judges," I heard the monitor say, "meet your next contestant—Miss Mississippi, Cheryl Prewitt."

Smiling, I entered the room and took my seat.

"Tell me, Miss Prewitt," said one man, in a tone more
suited to a courtroom cross-examiner than a pageant judge,
"who is one of Mississippi's most famous novelists?"

"Uh," I stammered, "James Faulkner? I mean, basically, at
least I think that's his name."

"Hm-m," the man responded. "No further questions."

From the corner of my eye, I could see Pat scrunching up
her eyes at me like a mole trapped in bright sunlight—obviously in gross imitation of what I must have looked like.

"Miss Prewitt!"

Turning to my right, I faced another man, whose stern expression indicated that he, for one, was taking this exercise
very seriously, indeed.

"It's common knowledge," he said, "that Mississippi has
produced many fine singers over the years—most of them
men. What I'd like to know is, what high-caliber woman art-
ist are you aware of?"

"I'm glad you asked that question," I replied—in truth not
glad at all, but stalling for time. In a desperate effort not to
close my eyes, I fixed what must have been a frighteningly

wall-eyed stare upon the man. "The answer you're looking for is Eudora Welty," I said.

Pat, who now seemed to be in a state of near-hysteria, was shaking her head wildly as if to cry out, "No, Cheryl, no!" I couldn't tell if it was my answer or my stare that had offended her.

"About this Eudora Welty," the man continued. "Can you tell me anything more about her?"

"Well," I said, remembering, as a last resort, to flash a brilliant smile, "I do believe the woman is an opera singer, is she not?"

Abruptly, the interview ended as the man collapsed with uncontrollable laughter, and the monitor stepped in to call, "Time!"

Returning to the kitchen, I felt my eyes fill with tears, my face flush with anger and embarrassment. *How could I have done so poorly? Why had I been so nervous?*

While leaving the room, I overheard one of the board members say to the others, "Don't you think you-all were a little hard on her?"

For a moment, there was no response. Then, the answer I heard took me by surprise.

"If you practice hard," a board member said, "the game's always easier."

With that, I realized that all my anger, nervousness, and embarrassment were nothing to be concerned about. In fact, to experience and overcome such feelings was the very purpose for the mock interviews. *Better that I flub up here and now,* I thought, *than later in Atlantic City.*

Blowing my nose and drying my eyes, I returned to the family room.

"Oh dear," said Pat, who must have sensed my distress. "I didn't think you'd take this all so seriously. You're among friends, you know. After all, Cheryl, this is supposed to be fun!"

"Fun?" I cried. "This was horrible! And you want to

know something else? Nothing in Atlantic City could ever be as horrible as this has been. *Nothing.*" Then, in spite of myself, I heard myself begin to chuckle. "Oh-h-h," I groaned, putting my hand to my forehead, "I can't believe how bad I was. Let's take a look at the playback and have a good laugh."

So that's what we did—later making a second videotape in which my performance was much improved.

As weeks passed, I became more and more adept at the videotaped sessions until, poised and confident, I actually began to look forward to them. Only one question continued to give me a hard time: at every mock interview, someone was sure to ask, "Tell me, Miss Prewitt, do you think you really will become the new Miss America?" And every time I answered, "I hope to be."

While no one criticized this response during the playbacks, I had the uneasy feeling it wasn't the answer they were looking for.

The one other remaining problem was getting my figure in shape for the upcoming Swimsuit competition. When I first modeled my swimsuit for Pat, she didn't mince any words about the matter.

"I guess you know you're going to have to lose some weight," she said. "You're heavy from the waist to the knees—especially around your upper thighs."

"I know," I moaned. "I've got those darn little paunches of fat. No matter how skinny I get, they just don't want to go away."

"Cellulite," said Pat definitively. "I'll have Briggs put you on a high-protein, low-calorie diet and exercise program. It may not be easy; you'll have to spot reduce, since you can't afford to lose much weight anywhere else."

"Easy or not, I've got no choice," I said. "If the press picks up on the story of my healing, I've got to have the best looking legs in town!"

"I hadn't thought of it that way," said Pat. "But you're absolutely right."

While it was easy enough for me to lose pounds (Jay helped me count calories, and Bubba ran laps with me around the high school track), ridding myself of those two small paunches of ugly fat proved to be next to impossible. Thus, it wasn't long before I found it necessary to follow a rigid daily regimen that went something like this:

8:00 A.M.—Up and at 'em! Don sweat suit (sometimes I used blue plastic knickers) and leg weights. Jog down two hundred–yard driveway to pick up morning newspapers. Return to house.

8:00–9:00—Fix breakfast: coffee with skim milk, Sweet 'n Low. Hook myself up to vibrating machine (kept in the family room) and jiggle for one hour, at same time reading morning papers from front to back, making sure to note and memorize significant current events.

9:00–10:00—Hop aboard stationary bicycle (also kept in the family room) and pedal twelve miles, at same time watching and studying TV morning news and talk shows for interview information.

10:00–11:00—Return to vibrating machine and jiggle for another hour, at same time reading and studying current periodicals and state and national information fact sheets.

11:00–2:00 P.M.—Fix lunch: hard-boiled egg or apple. Don swimsuit and bake till brown in backyard sun. (Good-bye, quick-tanning lotion!)

2:00–3:00—Return to stationary bicycle for another twelve-mile ride, this time spending the hour in contemplative prayer.

3:00–4:00—Return to vibrating machine, this time with my Bible, for an hour of quiet (save for the hum of the machine) scripture study.

Following a high-protein supper, evenings were filled for the most part with more mock interviews at the house or

Talent rehearsals and Swimsuit and Evening Gown walk-throughs at the local high school auditorium stage.

11:00–12:00—Return to stationary bicycle for the day's final ride.

12:00 midnight—Collapse into bed, exhausted.

As demanding as such a schedule was, it occurred to me at some point that never again would I have the opportunity to so single-mindedly indulge in getting myself in near-perfect shape—not only physically, but mentally and spiritually, too. This, in fact, was my sole responsibility in preparing for the Miss America Pageant. And for this reason it became easy for me to stick to my regimen with a relentless sense of duty and discipline.

One afternoon as I was jiggling on the vibrating machine and reading my Bible, I came across the passage about faith that Madelyn had mentioned so long ago: "Now faith is the assurance of things hoped for, the conviction of things not seen" (Hebrews 11:1 RSV). It was, I recalled somewhat wistfully, the spiritual principle that had enabled Doyle Blackwood to find as much joy in the act of praying as in the results he hoped for. Still, the passage left me feeling puzzled and vaguely dissatisfied.

Even now, having won the title of Miss Mississippi and believing in my heart that I was going to win Miss America, the deep joy of certain knowing—the kind of joy I knew that Doyle had experienced—had so far eluded me. No matter how much I believed in my heart and confessed with my mouth that I was going to win, there remained a tiny part of my spirit that was still subject to fleeting doubts and fears. While Madelyn had predicted that I would some day have Doyle's kind of faith, I still found the concept hard to grasp.

"Help me, Lord," I prayed quietly, as I turned off the machine and let the strap fall from my hips. "Help me have the kind of faith that Doyle had."

That evening, a group of pageant board members were coming over for yet another videotaped mock interview.

Over time, I'd grown to look forward to not only the sessions, but also to the people who volunteered so many hours of their time to help out. Often, their selfless dedication amazed me. I appreciated their efforts more than they could ever know.

This time the mock interview proceeded in what had come to be typically smooth fashion—save for the one troublesome question.

Again, I was asked, "Do you think, Miss Prewitt, that you will be the next Miss America?"

And again, I answered, "Well sir, I hope to be."

Later, after watching the videotape playback, the subject finally came up.

"You're doing splendidly," said Briggs. "And you're getting better every day. Right now, Cheryl, I'd say you've got as good a chance as any girl to win the title. There's only one answer I think you could improve on."

"I know the one you mean," I said. "I've sensed all along you've been looking for something more than I've been giving you."

"Tell me," Briggs said with a smile, "do you actually want to win the title?"

"Yes," I replied, "of course I do."

"Do you think you're going to win?" he asked.

"I know I am," I said. "At least, that's what I've been confessing since January."

"Well, great!" he exclaimed. "If that's how you feel, then say so! When someone asks you if you think you're going to win, don't say, 'Well, I hope so.' State the truth: say you *know* so!" He laughed. "Let's run through it once," he suggested, "just to see how it feels."

Clearing his throat, Briggs looked me straight in the eye, and said, "Tell me, Miss Prewitt, do you think you're going to be the next new Miss America?"

"Yes sir," I replied. "I do. I want to win the title, and I know I'm going to."

No sooner had the words left my mouth when I thought my heart might burst with happiness. What I had just said, I realized, was more than a rehearsed answer to a tough interview question; it was absolute *truth!* In a very real way, I was as happy and certain now as I knew I was going to be when Bert Parks announced my name as winner in Atlantic City. It was almost as though I had already won the title—it just hadn't happened yet in time and space.

Later that night as I dropped off to sleep it occurred to me that what I had experienced was more than the cumulative effects of positive thinking; it was positive *knowing.* It was, simply, full-power faith—the kind of faith that Paul wrote about in Hebrews 11:1, the kind of faith that Doyle had, the kind of faith that I'd so long been praying for.

"Thank You, Father," I whispered, as I closed my eyes. "Thank You for Your gift of faith. Let me always use it to Your glory. In Jesus' name I pray—amen."

With the problem of my troublesome interview question solved, only one more difficulty remained: the stubborn paunches of fat on my thighs.

But as if in confirmation of the powerful surge of faith I had experienced, that problem was solved, too—not too many days later.

Oddly enough, it happened overnight; that is, one day the paunches were there, the next day gone. When I modeled my swimsuit for Pat, she couldn't believe her eyes.

"It's incredible!" she exclaimed. "You've been working for weeks to get rid of those bulges and now—in one day—they're gone! I've never seen anything like it." She laughed. "You look fantastic."

"I feel fantastic," I said. "Body, mind, spirit—I've never felt so good in all my life. Look out, world," I grinned, striking a playful beauty-queen pose, "Atlantic City, here I come!"

IT WAS SATURDAY AFTERNOON, September 1, when Pat and I arrived in Atlantic City, New Jersey. Also checking in at the Bala Motor Inn where we would be staying were contestants from five other states—all girls who Pat considered to be top contenders for the title of Miss America.

"You know," said Pat, as she began unpacking her bags for our week-long stay, "I've got a funny feeling that the winner's going to be coming from this hotel."

"You better believe it," I said. "In fact, she's going to be coming right from this room!"

My confidence hadn't diminished in the least over our fifteen-hundred-mile journey from Vicksburg. While I'd never been so far away from home (and never so far north!), I still felt entirely in my element. Deep in my heart, I remained convinced that God was going to have me win; He wasn't about to let me go out on a limb and then saw it off behind me.

Later, when I tried to explain my certainty about winning in long-distance phone calls to Becky Curtis and Pam Williams (who were not able to make the trip), they didn't understand. Not wanting me to be hurt if I lost, they warned me not to get my hopes up too high and to be happy with how far I'd come.

Often I longed for a few quiet moments with Madelyn, who I thought was probably the one person who might understand. But due to pageant rules, I was not permitted to visit with her—or any of the more than one hundred others who had made the trip to Atlantic City from Mississippi, by train, plane, and chartered bus. Everyone, it seemed, was here; Mother and Daddy, Madelyn, Aunt Dot and Uncle James, Uncle Doyle Tennyson (another of Mother's brothers), Briggs and Pat, Sara and Bill Foster, Paulette, Tim,

Heath, William—even Lavez Blackwood. The only person whose presence I missed was Doyle.

Though I couldn't enjoy everyone's company face to face, I could feel the heat of their prayers holding me up, bolstering my faith, fueling me with energy.

From the first day our fact sheets were distributed, the press picked up on my story. When they asked me for details, I told them all I knew. Soon, in local papers, small articles began to appear about "Miss Mississippi and her miraculous healing."

One curious result of this early publicity was that it caused Christian contestants, of which there were several (Miss Florida, Miss Louisiana, Miss Tennessee, Miss Kentucky, and Miss Oklahoma, to name a few) to seek me out for fellowship. Frequently, during rehearsal breaks, we chatted and sometimes prayed together. Often we laughed at the fact that all of us were praying to win. "Now how," we joked, "does God propose to handle that?"

Caught up in rehearsals and preliminary judgings, the first part of the week flew by. It was fun being a contestant. Relaxed and confident in my interviews with judges, I sensed that they were a tremendous success. And on Friday night, when I won the Swimsuit preliminary, I was more encouraged than ever.

By Saturday night, the evening of the big pageant, I was high as a kite with confidence. Never mind that a contestant's chances for winning—as stated by Bert Parks when the telecast began—were one in seventy thousand. Never mind, too, the fact that my television microphone went dead as I left my piano and stood to finish "Don't Cry Out Loud." In less than a second, the power returned and I was in hog-heaven performing for the largest audience I'd ever known—twenty-five thousand in house and an estimated 100 million in homes across the country.

And when it came time for me to walk across the stage in

my swimsuit, I felt fabulous. Never better. To judges and press alike, who were by now all aware of my healing, I thought, *Anyone who's had any doubts about my story, just look at these legs. Look at them! They're great. They're perfect. They're living proof that God, in His love and power, can take the most crippled legs and transform them into something beautiful.*

Near the end of the program, as Bert Parks was in the process of announcing the fourth through first runner-ups, he almost slipped and accidently revealed the top winner's name.

No! I thought, nearly crying the warning out loud. *Please don't make a mistake! Please don't ruin my big moment!*

I was that sure that I was going to win.

Nonetheless, at the very last moment, I remembered to pray my pageant prayer: *Lord,* I said silently, *if I can do more good for You—reach more people—as Miss America than as Miss Mississippi, then let me win. Otherwise, don't.*

It was seconds later that I at last heard those long-awaited words: "Ladies and gentlemen, here she is—Miss America 1980—Cheryl Prewitt!"

I wasn't shocked. I didn't cry. But oh, I was so happy. Happier than I'd ever been in all my life.

"Thank you," I said to the judges, who were seated in a gallery below the runway. "Thank you," I called to the wildly cheering audience. "Oh thank you, everyone!" I glanced upward to the ceiling of the huge auditorium from whose lofty heights God surely must have been enjoying the scene.

Suddenly, like something from out of a dream, Bert Parks, in his mellow, supper-club tenor, burst into his classic rendition of the Miss America theme song. Red roses and gleaming scepter were placed in my hands, a sparkling crown upon my head. A gentle push, and I was off, gliding down a light-lined runway that reminded me for all the world of a landing strip at midnight—and which seemed at least half as long.

Halfway through my walk, it suddenly occurred to me that had I allowed Satan to fill my heart with doubt and fear, not only would I not have won, but I could easily have been spending tonight at home in a wheelchair, watching the pageant on television. But encouraged by a wonderful family and so many friends, I had chosen instead to believe in my Father and His truths. That was why I was here. The only reason why.

Now, I did begin to cry.

"Thank you, thank you," I repeated over and over again to the cameras and to the audience. "I love you, I love you." Though blinded by the spotlights, in my mind's eye I could see everyone's faces clearly—even those of Becky and Pam, who were watching the pageant at home. I wanted so much to reach out and touch them, hold them, let them know how happy and grateful I was and how much I loved them.

At some point, the TV cameramen began motioning for me to hurry up, to walk faster and return to the stage. But I would not hurry. I would not diminish what represented to me the culmination of a lifetime of prayers and effort—not only my own, but those of countless others.

Once the house lights had been turned on and the auditorium began to clear, a small press conference took place. It was very brief (the major press conference was to take place in New York City, two days later) and the questions, for the most part, were friendly and typical: "How do you feel right now?" "Did you think you were going to win?" "Do you have a boyfriend?" "What do you plan to do when your reign ends?"

Suddenly, however, the questions became focused on the subject of my healing. Albeit skeptical, the press seemed at the same time fascinated by the story—barraging me with questions ranging from "What religion are you?" to "When, exactly, did this so-called miracle take place?" I answered everything the best I could, praying throughout that God would somehow be glorified by what I said.

Later, when the floodlights had been turned off and TV camera crews and reporters were packing up their equipment, Miss Florida, Marty Phillips (who had placed fourth runner-up in the pageant), came running toward me, tears streaming down her face. I hadn't seen her since we'd been together on stage earlier in the evening.

"Marty," I said. "What's wrong?"

"Oh, Cheryl," she cried, throwing her arms around me, "I prayed tonight to God that I'd win—but that if He could be better glorified by someone else, that she would win. It was such a noble prayer," she laughed, "and to tell the truth, when I didn't win, I wasn't much comforted by it. But now, after seeing the way you handled that press conference, after hearing your testimony—now I know why you're the one who won! Oh, Cheryl, I'm so happy for you—and for all the good that's going to come from your reign as Miss America!"

"Oh, Marty," I said, "those are the most wonderful words I've heard all evening. Thanks for sharing them with me. I'm going to remember this moment forever."

"I'll be praying for you," said Marty, hugging me tightly. "All year long."

"And me, for you, too," I said.

With barely enough time to dab my tear-stained eyes and touch up my lipstick, I was off to the Miss America Coronation Ball, which also took place in the Convention Hall. Escorted into the huge room by the President of the Miss America Pageant, I was reunited with my family for the first time in what seemed like a year.

To my dismay, everyone (with the exception of Heath, who was too busy sampling hors d'oeuvres and inspecting my crown) was crying.

"What's all this about?" I asked, feeling my own eyes begin to fill with tears. "You're supposed to be happy!"

Mother, too overcome to speak, just shook her head.

"We're gonna miss you," said Paulette. "That's all. We're happy for you, but it's also kind of like we're losing you—you know what I mean?"

"Losing me?" I cried. "Never!" I turned to Daddy, so handsome in his best dress suit. "What are they talking about?" I asked.

"Well," he responded with a wistful smile, "I think your mother would have been happier had you come in as first runner-up." He grinned. "Come to think of it, maybe I would've, too."

"Daddy!" I cried. "Don't say that!"

"Honey," he said, "You know very well that I believe it's God's will that you won tonight. You did what you had to do. Now you just be sure to live up to the big job He's given you, hear?"

"Oh, Daddy," I said, "I will. You know I will."

"Yes," he said, hugging me tightly. "I know you will. We'll all be praying for you, too."

It was four in the morning when Pat and I returned to our room—this time the palatial "Miss America Suite" at Atlantic City's Caesars Boardwalk Regency.

"Gosh," I said, as I set my crown down on what was the biggest bed I'd ever seen. "You mean I get to sleep on this all by myself?"

"There's another bed over here," called Pat, from a distant part of the suite. "And a sitting room, and a bathroo—" Suddenly she gasped. "Oo-oh, Cheryl, come here and take a look at this tub!"

"Oh, no!" I cried, as I joined Pat to gawk at an immense pink-tiled, heart-shaped, sunken bath. I giggled. "It reminds me of the ads for honeymoon resorts in the back pages of brides' magazines," I said. "Guess I'd better take a good long look—may not see one again for a long time!" I laughed.

For some reason, the situation made me think of Doyle. The tub, for all its extravagance, was so silly! *How Doyle would have laughed*, I thought, *could he have been with us.*

"Thank You, Father," I murmured a short while later as I drifted off to sleep. "Thank You so much for all the wonderful events of this past evening. And Father—if it's true that You delight in letting Your children up in Heaven know about all the good things that happen to their loved ones here on earth—please let Doyle know about tonight. I know it would make him so happy."

Two hours later I was up at the crack of dawn, slipping into a shorts outfit for a 7:00 A.M. photo session on the chilly Atlantic City beach. I could hardly wait to be finished and get to the Miss America Breakfast, where I would be able to be with my family. Our time together the night before had been so brief and confused; this would be my last chance to talk and say good-bye before embarking on my year-long itinerary of public appearances.

But when I arrived at the breakfast (which also took place at the Convention Hall) my family was not there.

"I'm sorry," one of the pageant officials explained, "but your folks left for home early this morning. I thought you knew."

"No," I said, slightly confused. "No, I didn't."

"Well," he said, "there was so much excitement last night."

"Um-hm," I agreed vaguely. "Yes, there was."

I tried not to let show on my face the sickening feeling of homesickness that had suddenly twisted my stomach into a hard knot. My eyes burned with tears. Everyone had gone! I was all alone! It was as though the world had fallen away from me. I felt lost. Scared. Not happy at all about the prospect of three hundred sixty-five days on the road as Miss America, I wanted to go home!

Suddenly, as I gazed out over the sea of tables and the hundreds of strangers milling around and finding their places, it occurred to me that this was the way my life was going to be from here on out; this, in essence, was what being Miss America was all about. I was on my own now and had better face up to it. Moreover, I had a job to do. It was my job to meet these strangers—here, and the world over—and make them my friends. It was my job to share with them the love and blessings that so graciously had been showered upon me in my lifetime. Besides, I wasn't really alone. With Jesus, I was never really alone . . .

Suddenly, I heard someone calling my name.

Looking out over the crowd of faces I saw, of all people, my Aunt Dot. Aunt Dot—the person who had, from the start, encouraged me to never give up. Aunt Dot—most definitely not a stranger!

"Aunt Dot!" I cried. "What are you doing here? I thought everyone had gone home!"

"Well," she said, "I got to thinking last night what a pity it would be to leave this place without saying a decent good-bye, so I booked a flight home for later this afternoon. You sure do look pretty, Cheryl. How're you doing?"

"Oh, Aunt Dot," I cried, "I'm so happy. Especially to see you. You've made me so happy!"

"Me?" she asked.

"Yes, you," I said. "I love you so much—*so* much!"

"Well," said Aunt Dot, "I love you, too. Always have, you know. Let's be sure to get together later, once this breakfast is over—all right?"

"Great," I said. "See you then."

"Oh, Father," I murmured under my breath as I watched Aunt Dot make her way back to her seat. "Thank You for sending Aunt Dot to be here today, when I needed her so badly. Thank You for taking such good care of me."

Though Aunt Dot couldn't know it, her appearance at the breakfast had been, for me, a wonderful symbol of God's love—the love that promised to hold me and my family to-gether forever, no matter how far I traveled, no matter how long I stayed away.

IT WAS SUNDAY EVENING, and I was dining with Mr. and Mrs. Albert Marks in the dimly lit restaurant of midtown Manhattan's elegant Barclay Hotel. Mr. Marks was chairman of the board for the Miss America Pageant, Inc., the Atlantic City–based corporation which oversees the annual pageant from its grass-root beginnings on up.

We'd arrived in New York City early that afternoon, and since then (between my gazing in wonder at the mile-high skyscrapers and seemingly endless lines of yellow taxis) Mr. Marks had more or less taken me under his wing, using the time to explain to me all that would be involved in my coming year as Miss America.

For starters, I would be earning anywhere from $20,000 to $80,000, depending on the number of bookings obtained by my Miss America staff manager and other sources such as my family. Primary bookings would include appearances and advertisements for the Gillette and Kellogg companies, who were pageant sponsors; other bookings would range from opening shopping centers to singing in churches in much the same way as I had done with my family. In addition, there would be television appearances, a meeting with the President at the White House, and a one-month summer tour of the Far East with the Miss America USO entertainment troupe. Throughout, I would be accompanied by an official Miss America chaperone, one of two women who took one-month turns at the job.

In the course of the day, Mr. and Mrs. Marks and I had become old friends. I especially appreciated Mr. Marks for his candor and for his obvious concern that I felt comfortable and prepared for my new position.

"The most important thing," he was saying to me now, as the three of us chatted over coffee and dessert, "is to be yourself. Do that, and you'll make out just fine."

"Thanks, Mr. Marks," I said. "I'm so grateful for every-thing you've told me today. I really do feel very good about the job."

"Well, we feel good about you, too," he smiled. "That, I imagine, is the reason why you won." He paused, thought-fully stirring his coffee. "There's one more thing we really should talk about—and that's tomorrow's New York press conference. It's scheduled to take place here, at the Barclay, at ten A.M. Everyone will be here—all the major television networks, wire services, syndicated and local press. They could be tough on you, and I just wanted to warn you."

"Warn me?" I said, not liking at all the distinctly ominous tone that had suddenly entered our conversation.

"I'm afraid so," said Mr. Marks. "In fact, as Miss America, this New York press conference could very well be your most difficult task."

"How so?" I asked.

"Well," said Mr. Marks, "as I'm sure you're well aware, in recent years the pageant has come under some criticism; there are those who feel it's not only an outdated idea, but exploitative of women."

"Not me," I said. "I think pageants are great. From my ex-perience, they serve to build a person's confidence, they award millions of dollars in scholarships—why, they can work to change a person's life. Besides, the Miss America Pageant is an American institution!"

"I agree!" grinned Mr. Marks. "Tell that to the press!" Leaning back in his chair, he continued. "The other thing they may give you a hard time with is this story about your miraculous healing. Traditionally, see, the press doesn't want to hear things like that. They want facts. They want logical explanations. Unfortunately, religion and miracles don't set well with that kind of mind-set."

"I see," I said. "They're of the opinion that Christianity is some sort of emotional phenomenon—unscientific, irrational, and—above all—nonintellectual. That Christians as a whole are a group of simple-minded, self-righteous do-gooders."

"You might say that," said Mr. Marks.

"Well," I said, "I'm glad you brought this up. Do you have any suggestions?"

"Like I said before," said Mr. Marks, "be yourself. Say what you know to be true. Stand up for what you believe. But remember this: whatever you stand up for, be sure you're able to back it up."

"Well, that should be easy enough," I said. "When it comes to my healing, all they have to do is look at my legs."

Mr. Marks sighed. "I wish, for your sake, it were going to be that easy."

The next morning found me waking up more than a little nervous about the upcoming press conference. After considering Mr. Marks's advice, I was beginning to hope that perhaps the press might totally ignore the story of my healing and stick to questions about women's rights and the like. I could save my Christian testimony for the churches; after all, now that I was Miss America, I was sure to be appearing in a lot of them.

The more I thought about my strategy, however, the more uneasy I felt. Hadn't Jesus Himself commanded believers to "Go into all the world and preach the gospel" (Mark 16:15 RSV), not to hide our light under a bushel (Matthew 5:15, Mark 4:21, Luke 8:16, 11:33), to be like the light of the world, like a city on a hill (Matthew 5:14), and, moreover, not to be ashamed of Him and of His words (Mark 8:38)? Besides, hadn't my whole reason for becoming Miss America been to serve God by using the position as a means of spreading the good news of His love and reality in today's world?

As ten o'clock approached, it became clear to me that to try to skirt the issue of my healing would be the worst possible thing I could do. Nervous and insecure as I felt, I knew I'd have to go through with it.

Claiming the promise of Jesus as recorded in Matthew 10:19 RSV: "... do not be anxious how you are to speak or what you are to say; for what you are to say will be given to you [by the Holy Spirit] in that hour," I drew a deep breath and entered the elevator that would take me to the press conference.

The room, jam-packed with reporters and technicians, was bright as day with hot floodlights.

Lord, I prayed silently, as I made my way to the makeshift platform from where I'd be fielding questions, *this is Your press conference. I'm turning the whole thing over to You; please use me to Your glory.*

No sooner had I stepped to the podium when one particularly grumpy-looking reporter raised his hand and said, "Miss Prewitt, we think it's great that you've been crowned the new Miss America. But what's this we hear about God working a miracle in your life? Something about a childhood accident and doctors saying you'd never walk again?"

"That's right," I said, with a calmness that surprised me. "When I was a little girl, eleven years old, my life could have ended—but thanks to God, it didn't. After eight months of prayer and positive thinking, I was up and walking."

"But what's this we hear about a short leg being lengthened by a faith healer?"

"Ah," I smiled, "that's an even better story!" And with a quiet confidence and deep conviction I knew was coming from the Holy Spirit within me, I related my tale.

As I spoke, a wonderful thing began to happen. Incredibly, faces that had been hardened by years of skepticism began to soften into those belonging more to curious children. Hardly hostile, the press was fascinated!

"Now I'm not demanding that any of you believe my story," I said, as the hour-long conference—in what had seemed like minutes—drew to a close. "But remember, you're the ones who asked. If you can believe what I've told you, that's wonderful. If you can't—well, I only hope it's not because you think I'm not telling the truth, but rather because it's something you simply can't accept for yourself."

Moments later the conference was over. Lights were dimmed, tape recorders turned off, and technicians and reporters began packing up their equipment.

As someone reached up to help me down from the platform, I wondered what everyone was thinking. I wondered if any of them had felt just a touch of truth to what I'd said. I wondered if, in any way, God had somehow been glorified.

Just as I was about to exit, I got my answer.

"You know," I overheard one reporter saying to another, "it's the darndest thing. To hear her speak, she could almost make a believer out of me!"

Epilogue

About the Author

The remarkable story of Cheryl Prewitt's struggle to become Miss America 1980 has not lessened in impact since it was originally revealed to the public several years ago.

In the crowning year of her reign, the "little girl from Mississippi" went on to become one of the most talked-about winners in the history of the Miss America Pageant. In press conferences, speaking engagements, public appearances, and the myriad other duties revolving around the pageant, Cheryl never once lost her desire to make use of her incredible personal experience to share with others the good news of Jesus Christ.

In fact, within a year after she was crowned as Miss America, Cheryl began work on her first album, "I'm a Miracle," the release of which set off a whirlwind ministry. Neither she nor America has been the same since. In 1983 she recorded "Desires of My Heart," followed a year later by "Ain't Nothing Gonna Stop You Now," a lively, upbeat album which draws on the vibrant energy so characteristic of Cheryl's entire life and ministry.

Making the first of several decisions to "go against the grain" of industry practice and standards, Cheryl began to include in her albums and concerts motivational messages in which she presented the reality of Jesus Christ in a way understandable to people in every walk of life.

This new thrust was instrumental in the conception and creation of "Choose to Be Happy," a landmark album for Cheryl which helped focus her life and ministry on children and young adults. Anyone who has ever attended one of Cheryl's meetings can testify that it only takes five minutes to perceive that she has a special anointing for ministry to youngsters and a genuine concern for their precious hopes and dreams.

As the decade of the eighties reached its midpoint, it was evident that the Lord was moving Cheryl into a ministry not only of music, but also of healing. In meeting after meeting, she began to reach out to those in physical, mental and spiritual distress, and to see the Lord respond with amazing results.

The first time this type of supernatural manifestation took place in one of Cheryl's meetings was in a concert she was presenting. The Lord spoke to her and gave her a "word of knowledge" about one of the people in the audience. After having spent a lifetime in the rigorous self-discipline of piano lessons, drama rehearsals, and voice practice, the concept of freely "flowing in the Spirit" was not one to which Cheryl was accustomed. She held the word within herself until the next night when the impression became more specific.

Cheryl remembers that during the concert the next evening she saw in her spirit "a lady in a red dress with blue flowers on it." Cheryl stopped the music, bit her lip, then decided to take the plunge — she spoke out her impression. The lady was actually in the audience. When she stepped forward at Cheryl's request, she was instantly healed.

Many more such occurrences were to take place in her meetings before Cheryl was entirely comfortable with flowing in the anointing of a healing ministry. However, once she had learned to trust her spiritual insight enough to recognize Christ's leading within, her entire ministry was revolutionized. Today, churches across the nation are asking Cheryl to sing and share her experiences with their congregations.

In January 1985, Cheryl became a regular on the "Richard Roberts Live" daily television show. Seen in almost every major city in America, the program has opened Cheryl's life — her ministry, testimony, and experience — to millions of people who had not seen or heard of her since the Miss America Pageant. The remarkable amount of mail she receives in response to the show reflects her ability to reach out to people on all levels of life, but especially to housewives and homemakers who are able to see the program during the day.

Cheryl is also an excellent complement to the ministry of Richard Roberts, who has grown up in the healing ministry and who has given her valuable insight as she ministers through the unique medium of television.

After moving to Tulsa in 1985, Cheryl met and married Harry Salem, Executive Vice-President for Oral Roberts Ministries. On March 21, 1986, she gave birth to a wonderful son (called "Li'l Harry") who already has his sights on a football career!

Cheryl and her family are now living in a surburban area of the city, marking a new beginning in Cheryl's life and ministry. Not long ago she finished writing a mini-book, *Choose To Be Happy*, (published by Harrison House and available in local bookstores) which deals with the topic of self-image. In this book, Cheryl describes her experience of recovering physically, mentally and spiritually from a tragic auto accident in which she was badly injured as a child. This experience has given her a special vision and concern for people who suffer from low self-esteem.

Through her many television appearances, including appearing on the All-American Beauty Search Pageant, and serving with Pat Boone as co-host of the 1985 Dove Music Awards, Cheryl has a rare opportunity to reach both Christian and secular audiences in a way few people can. And in her experiences, Cheryl has found that poor self-image is prevalent in almost every group she has encountered. In response to this need, she has devoted a great deal of time and effort to helping people understand and develop their God-given potential. Through a program of positive faith, Cheryl seeks to build a foundation for a positive self-image by instilling and developing in every individual the perfect picture that God has in His mind of each of His beloved children.

(Since Cheryl stays with a task until it's truly finished, in the future you can expect to see a number of books by Cheryl on the subject of self-image.)

Perhaps the most exciting project Cheryl has developed in the recent past is her new home video production entitled, "Take Charge of Your Life with Cheryl and Friends." In an age when attention is given to health and fitness, Cheryl wanted to make use of her extraordinary abilities to produce a special aerobic video designed to develop a positive mental, emotional and spiritual awareness.

Cheryl believes that everyone has a choice to make, and that each person can *take charge* of his or her own life and be the success they have always dreamed of being! In one of the most professionally produced home videos on the market today, Cheryl takes the viewer through a 45-minute workout with special emphasis on the development of a winning attitude and a desire to be the best he or she can be in every circumstance of life.

This exciting home video production is available in local Christian bookstores.

The greatest part of Cheryl's life began the moment Bert Parks placed the Miss America crown on her head and she began the exhilarating walk down that flashbulb-laced runway in Atlantic City. God has really answered her prayer of commitment, "Lord, if You can use me better as Miss America than as Miss Mississippi, then I'm ready." In the years since the electric moment marking the fulfillment of her dream of becoming Miss America, this young woman has influenced the lives of countless thousands of people across this nation because of her willingness to take the way of the cross rather than the road of fame and fortune.

Today Cheryl's story is still being written. In churches and auditoriums, from recording studios and sound stages, on television screens and city street corners, the message of the Gospel of Jesus Christ is reaching the hearts of hurting, lost people because one young girl said yes to the call of God upon her life.

Cheryl understands the depth and darkness of despair because she has experienced it. But as she was lying in a hospital bed in Mississippi with a crushed leg, a slashed face, and a life of broken dreams, she took a moment to realize that this was only a beginning point — a God Who could heal a crushed leg and a torn face, could also heal those shattered dreams.

If you or someone you know can use the encouragement or hope that Cheryl can give, don't hesitate to contact her today. She would love to hear from you. To correspond with her, or to inquire about her albums and new video projects, write:

Cheryl Prewitt-Salem
P. O. Box 70128
Tulsa, OK 74170

Please include your prayer requests and comments when you write.

Books By
Cheryl Prewitt-Salem

A Bright-Shining Place

_____

Choose To Be Happy

Available from your local bookstore.

Harrison House
P. O. Box 35035
Tulsa, OK 74153